PROTECTING RIGHTS
in BRITAIN

Duncan Watts

Series Editor: David Simpson

Hodder & Stoughton
A MEMBER OF THE HODDER HEADLINE GROUP

ACKNOWLEDGEMENTS

The publishers would like to thank the following for granting permission to reproduce pictures in this book:

Topham Picture Point: page 13

Press Association/Topham: pages 45 and 46

Popperfoto/Reuters: page 81

Charter 88: page 101

Order queries: please contact Bookpoint Ltd, 39 Milton Park, Abingdon, Oxon OX14 4TD. Telephone: (44) 01235 400414, Fax: (44) 01235 400454. Lines are open from 9.00 - 6.00, Monday to Saturday with a 24 hour message answering service. Email address: orders@bookpoint.co.uk

A catalogue record for this title is available from The British Library

ISBN 0 340 711361

First published 1998
Impression number 10   9   8   7   6   5   4   3   2   1
Year   2002   2001   2000   1999   1998

Typeset by Transet Limited, Coventry, England.
Printed in Great Britain for Hodder & Stoughton Educational, a division of Hodder Headline plc, 338 Euston Road, London NW1 3BH by Redwood Books, Trowbridge, Wilts.

Cover Photograph by Image Net.

CONTENTS

PREFACE

A/AS Level syllabuses in Government and Politics aim to develop knowledge and understanding of the political system of the UK. They cover its local, national and European Union dimensions, and include comparative studies of aspects of other political systems, in order to ensure an understanding of the distinctive nature of the British political system. The minimum requirements for comparative study are aspects of systems with a separation of powers, how other systems protect the rights of individuals and how other electoral systems work.

Access to Politics is a series of concise topic books which cover the syllabus requirements, providing students with the necessary resources to complete the course successfully.

General advice on approaching exam questions

To achieve high grades you need to demonstrate consistency. Clearly address all parts of a question, make good use of essay plans or notes, and plan your time to cover all the questions.

Make your answers stand out from the crowd by using contemporary material to illustrate them. You should read a quality newspaper and listen to or watch appropriate programmes on radio and television.

Skills Advice

You should comprehend, synthesise and interpret political information in a variety of forms:

- Analyse and evaluate political institutions, processes and behaviour, political arguments and explanations.
- Identify parallels, connections, similarities and differences between aspects of the political systems studied.
- Select and organise relevant material to construct arguments and explanations leading to reasoned conclusions.
- Communicate the arguments with relevance, clarity and coherence, using vocabulary appropriate to the study of Government and Politics.

David Simpson

1

INTRODUCTION

HUMAN RIGHTS ARE those entitlements which allow us the minimum necessary conditions for a proper existence. In other words, they enable us to develop as individuals and achieve our potential irrespective of the class, ethnic background, nationality, religion or sex to which we belong.

THE NATURE OF HUMAN RIGHTS

The concept of human rights is an elusive one which is interpreted differently by different politicians and by different governments. Some place the emphasis on one set of rights, others stress the importance of different ones. Many writers would make a distinction between:

1 **Legal rights**: these are those liberties which the law allows us, and which are recognised by the judicial machinery in any state (eg: freedom of speech and freedom of assembly).
2 **Moral or natural rights**: sometimes these are described as inalienable rights, for these are entitlements which cannot or should not be removed for they derive from people's common humanity – a person ought to be granted them, because he or she has a morally compelling claim. They are inherited at birth, and are the sole property of the citizen who decides how and to what ends they are used. For centuries, political thinkers have discussed the existence of such rights and argued over how they can be recognised and made effective.

Legal rights are often based upon moral ones, especially in liberal democracies. Moral rights have been enumerated by many philosophers and in many documents (see below). John Locke, a leading political philosopher of the seventeenth century, wrote of the right to 'life, liberty and property': Thomas Jefferson, a founding father of the modern USA, listed 'life, liberty and the pursuit of happiness' as primary concerns; the Universal Declaration of Human Rights adopted by the United Nations states in Article 3 that everyone 'has the right to life, liberty and the security of the person'. Of the 30 Articles in that document, another (4) proclaims that no person 'shall be held in slavery or servitude', another (13) that everyone 'has the right to freedom of movement'. The spirit of that Declaration is laid down at the beginning, in Article 1 which observes that:

All human beings are born free and equal in dignity and rights. They are endowed with reason and conscience, and should act toward one another in a spirit of brotherhood.

FAMOUS DECLARATIONS OF BASIC RIGHTS

The American Declaration of Independence (1776) proclaimed that 'all men...are endowed by the Creator with certain inalienable rights'. It went on to list these, and spoke of 'life, liberty and the pursuit of happiness' as foremost amongst them.

The French adopted the Declaration of the Rights of Man and Citizens in 1789, and it asserted that:

Men are born free and equal in rights...the aim of every political association is the preservation of the natural and undoubted rights of men. These rights are liberty, property, security and resistance to oppression.

After the Second World War, there was a mood of idealism in which peoples among the world community felt that the horror and devastation of the past must be no more. A new era of peace, brotherhood and respect for the rights of man was envisaged, and the commitment to human freedoms was a reflection of this concern for a better future.

Against this background, in 1948, the Universal Declaration of Human Rights was adopted by the UN, and it recognised that; 'The inherent dignity and ... the equal and inalienable rights of all members of the human family is the foundation of freedom, justice and peace in the world'. Accordingly all, human beings,

regardless of race, colour, sex, language, religion, political or other opinion, national or social origin, property, birth or other status are entitled to those freedoms laid down in the Declaration.

This was an attempt to set out standards of behaviour to which all states should aspire. Civilised nations were expected to obey the code laid down in the document, but if they did not do so voluntarily there was no way of enforcing their compliance. In effect, an individual had no satisfactory redress, if his or her rights were violated.

As we have seen, legal rights derive from our membership of a particular society rather than from our status as human beings. They will vary from country to country, and there is no limit to their number. Different governments concede different rights, and at any time they can be amended or removed by a change in the law. For our purposes, a useful division is between:

1 **Civil and political rights**, which are the minimum ones necessary for full citizenship.
2 **Economic and social rights**, which cover the living standards and lifestyle of people who live in the community.

The rights which people can enjoy are usually outlined in the constitution or fundamental law of the state. Some are of the moral/natural variety, most are civil or political. They are entitlements which are deemed to be essential if legal, political and social life is to operate effectively.

Writers often make the further distinction between **civil liberties** and **civil rights**. Civil liberties enable an individual to carry out certain actions which allow him or her to participate fully in the political system, for instance free speech and freedom of assembly. Civil rights are a set of protections which make people free from something which could otherwise greatly affect their lives (eg freedom from arbitrary arrest and imprisonment, or from discrimination on grounds of such things as gender, ethnic background or religion).

Different ideologies place greater emphasis on some rights and freedoms than on others. **Traditional socialists** have tended to stress the importance of collective rights which enable groups to work together to improve their position. For them, such rights as freedom of assembly and the right to take industrial action are particularly important. They argue that several of the civil and political rights have little real meaning without the addition of certain rights of an economic and social character. To be really free to do something implies having the means (ie the money, resources and opportunities) to do so. In other words, concern about rights involves doing something to remove the unfair differential between those who possess economic power and those who do not. The Blair leadership of the Labour Party places less emphasis on the importance of this concern for greater equality than some socialists would wish, but along with Liberal Democrats and others committed to an extension of civil rights, its spokespersons do argue the case for positive freedoms such as freedom from sexual or racial discrimination.

Conservatives place much emphasis on widening the area of choice available to individuals, and would argue for the right to determine the type of education available for children, the right to opt for private health provision, the right not to join a trade union, and particularly for the right to own and bequeath property. They generally prefer to see the government of the day doing less, passing fewer laws and not unduly interfering with people as they pursue their lives. In this view, the activities of government are circumscribed, and a traditional refrain is that the best government is that which governs least.

THE DEVELOPMENT OF RIGHTS CONSCIOUSNESS

In the postwar era there has been a growing interest in the area of human rights. Whereas for a long while the rights emphasised tended to require the government not to act (eg freedom of expression), in recent years more importance has been attached to the passage into law of entitlements which do need positive government intervention. Depending on the regime, government was expected – at the least – to be concerned about safeguarding the right to work, and to enjoy an adequate standard of living, decent accommodation, a fair income, educational and health opportunities. Many have seen it as the duty of government to promote such standards and opportunities by active intervention. Again, in the last generation, there has been a growing consensus that measures should be taken to enhance freedom from discrimination in many fields, on grounds such as disability, gender and race. In other words, in many societies thinking has moved on from concern with negative liberty – freedom from state interference – to a concern for positive liberty, the actual promotion of policies to advance people's rights.

This emergence of a growing concern for rights and for new types of rights has been reflected in many of the international conventions which have been devised dealing with the topic. The UN Universal Declaration of Human Rights (UNUDHR) adopted in 1948 stands as an ideal to which member nations should aspire, though the document has no legal status. By contrast, the UN International Covenant on Civil and Political Rights (ICCPR) which came into effect in 1966 is supposed to be binding on countries which have ratified it, as is the European Convention on Human Rights drawn up by the Council of Europe and in operation since 1953. The European Convention has done much to expand the liberty of the individual and the rights of minorities in member countries, and it has served as a benchmark for many activists concerned with rights across the world. In 1959, in New Delhi, an International Commission of Jurists urged all governments to seek inspiration from its contents and operation.

Other than in conventions, the emergence of 'rights consciousness' has been apparent in the development of new constitutions and/or of special provisions for the protection of rights. Several countries have introduced some form of charter or bill of rights. Countries which had previously been satisfied with the old 'Westminster model of democracy' began to contemplate new forms of protection; Canada and New Zealand have gone down this route. Countries granted independence by Britain in the postwar era have – with the single exception of Israel – all opted for a written constitution with a bill of rights to operate in tandem with it. In addition, in the US which has had such provision throughout its relatively short history, the Supreme Court has in the postwar era been noted for its 'judicial activism', seeing the protection and advancement of individual and minority rights as a major function.

Discussion of rights has been – and continues to be – much in the air. The developments noted around the world have been closely followed by enthusiasts for human rights everywhere, and in Britain those who have lamented the alleged inadequacy of our own provision have paid particular heed to the initiatives taken and practices in operation beyond our shores.

Liberties and rights are of especial concern to Britain and other liberal democracies which ought to possess a very broad range of them. The word 'liberalism' is associated with the primacy of the individual. Historically, liberal thinkers have always been committed to personal freedom, believing that men and women flourish and progress when they are able to express their creative personalities without undue restriction; liberals find the language of rights comes naturally to their lips. In democracies, governments are empowered by the people; they are given office on trust, and their power should not be abused. There may be occasions in which there is a need to deploy the police or security services, and to impose other limitations on freedom. But those restrictions must be capable of justification on grounds of the common good, and the more the citizens know of the reasoning behind them the better, for then they can assess whether essential values have been preserved. Liberal democratic societies everywhere should be characterised by a respect for human rights.

In other regimes, such a respect for basic liberties is often lacking, and there are many examples where individuals are appallingly abused. A few years ago, Algeria was not often mentioned as having a particularly poor record on human rights; however the Algerian Government is waging a war against Islamic fundamentalists, and any concern for decency has tended to be an early casualty. Blowtorching of the face and genitals, and other outrages against civilised values, have been documented in a report by Amnesty International, *Fear and Silence, a Hidden Human Rights Crisis*. Other instances abound, but this one achieved prominence soon after the Labour government took over in 1997. It served to highlight the brutality, torture and murder its spokespersons had condemned, and posed the first human rights test for the new Foreign Secretary. His earlier comment, suggesting that Britain had 'principles' abroad as well as 'interests', is an indication of the growing recognition given to issues of basic liberty in international affairs, as well as in the conduct of national policy. He promised to:

work through international forums and bilateral relationships to spread the values of human rights, civil liberties and democracy which we demand for ourselves.

AN OUTLINE OF THIS BOOK

In our study, we are primarily concerned with civil and political rights of the type defined in the Universal Declaration and in the European Convention on

Human Rights and Fundamental Freedoms. Our particular interest includes such things as police powers, prisoners' rights, freedom of association, of assembly and of speech, immigration and nationality, freedom from racial discrimination, women's rights, sexual orientation and the rights of minority groups such as the disabled. Civil liberties in the context of political violence such as terrorism are a further important area of enquiry.

Having defined our terms and explained what we understand by human rights, we can proceed to examine what rights we might reasonably expect, and why some people are troubled by some of the trends of the past generation and their implications for our traditional freedoms. A consideration of our international obligations and of the experience of other countries in the field of human rights will help us to assess the alternatives available, before considering in detail the case for a British bill of rights, and what it might mean for British citizens in practice.

Finally, a word of caution. When we speak of a bill of rights for Britain, we are not concerned with the one enacted in 1689. That legislation was introduced in the aftermath of the Glorious Revolution of the previous year, and was concerned primarily with the relationship of Parliament and the Crown. The type of bill referred to in this study is concerned with human rights and the provision of a document comprehensively enumerating them, as a basic part of our constitutional arrangements.

Make brief notes to remind you of:

1 The different types of rights to which people claim entitlement.
2 The factors which have helped promote a greater interest in and respect for rights in the post-war era.

Glossary

Civil liberties   A set of protections against governmental restrictions which enable an individual to carry out certain actions

Civil rights   A set of protections for individuals and groups which make them free from something, such as arbitrary arrest or discrimination

Inalienable rights   Those which should never be denied or taken away

2

THE RIGHTS COMMONLY CLAIMED

Introduction

SUPPORTERS OF DIFFERENT political ideologies place emphasis on different political freedoms. Those on the political Right tend to stress property rights, and the avoidance of needless governmental interference in the lives of the individual. Those on the Left are more sympathetic to collective rights, such as the opportunity to belong to a trade union. Hence the freedoms listed in the charters produced by campaigning bodies can be divergent.

In Britain, we have no definitive statement of our rights. The nearest thing to it is the European Convention, whose requirements we are obliged to follow. Our domestic protection relies on three 'pillars': Parliament, the culture of liberty and the courts. There is increasing support for the view that, even if these traditional remedies were once adequate, they are so no longer. The evidence of several writers in Britain and of some international research suggests that there are deficiencies in the British approach, and that more needs to be done if individuals are to be citizens rather than subjects.

Key Points
As you read this chapter, ask yourself:

- Which rights are important to you?
- How are they protected?
- Are our freedoms secure or can they be taken away?
- How does Britain fare in relation to the rest of the world?
- In what areas are there grounds for concern?

INDIVIDUAL LIBERTIES AND RIGHTS

The existence or absence of certain individual liberties and rights is the litmus test for a country which claims to be democratic. There may be disagreement over the freedoms to which citizens are entitled, but the following would command general assent:

- The right to life and personal security;
- equality before the law, and other legal freedoms such as freedom from inhuman or degrading punishment;
- The right to vote in free elections, on the basis of political equality;
- freedom of expression, including the right to speak and write freely, freedom of assembly and of movement, as well as freedom of information;
- freedom of conscience, including the right to worship or not to worship.

Some would claim freedom from discrimination and equal access to liberties which are associated with the idea of equality before the law. In more recent years, the right to privacy in the home, during recreation and in respect of correspondence is often asserted, as are a range of social rights. Concerning the main civil and political rights, there is only minor controversy. However, economic and social rights are a more contentious area.

LEGAL RIGHTS

Legal rights include not only the idea of **equality before the law** (the right of all citizens, whatever their background, gender, religion or race to be treated the same way). The right of **personal freedom** allowing everyone to act and behave as they would wish to do, subject to not breaking the law, is a long recognised and fundamental one. As far back as 1215, Magna Carta laid down the principle that:

No freeman shall be taken or imprisoned or disseised (dispossessed), nor will we go upon him nor will we send upon him except by the lawful judgement of his peers or (and) the law of the land.

Freedom from arbitrary arrest is protected by the ancient writ of Habeas Corpus, by which any detainee must be brought before a court within a specified time. Anyone held for a 'serious arrestable offence' must be produced before a magistrate after 36 hours. Given the authorisation of the magistrates, detention can be continued for up to a maximum of four days. However, under the Prevention of Terrorism Acts, regularly renewed since 1975, a person can be held for up to a maximum of seven days.

Once held in custody, the right to a **fair trial**, the presumption that a person is **innocent until proven guilty** and – give or take recent changes (see pp 47–48) – **the right of the accused to silence** are accepted features of our legal system.

SOCIAL RIGHTS

Among the social, economic and cultural rights which might be asserted are the following;

- the right to an adequate standard of living – food, clothing, accommodation etc;
- the right to work;
- the right to reasonable conditions of labour – fair hours and rates of pay, among them;
- protection against unemployment;
- the right to free education and access to higher education;
- the right to health care;
- special assistance for mothers and children.

In the area of social rights, there is much scope for disagreement. Many would assert the right to work, to housing, to health care and to decent educational opportunities. But difficulties abound. The right to work may be seen as a fundamental one, but what if – perhaps for sound reasons – the priorities of government policy concern the defeat of inflation and the curbing of state spending? This runs the risk of greater unemployment, and the right to work is then one denied to many people. The right of access to good health care and education is accepted as crucial, in that both help to determine life opportunities. But does that include the freedom to pay for private provision which may confer an extra advantage on those who have the means available? And what about housing? Everyone clearly needs shelter, but is it incumbent upon every individual to make his or her own arrangements or is there an entitlement to some form of public accommodation for those in need of a home?

The range of possible social rights is almost limitless. Some 20 years ago, the Institution of Professional Civil Servants agreed at its annual conference that the provision of a pension scheme which was inflation-proof, and therefore guaranteed a certain level of purchasing power, was a basic human right and principle of elementary justice.

Particularly controversial at the present time is the issue of abortion, a matter on which some alleged rights conflict with others. The right of a woman to have total control over her own body and thus have an abortion should she so wish is asserted by the 'pro-choice' lobby. This is not consistent with the wishes of 'pro-lifers' who argue for the right to life of the unborn foetus, a potential human being.

There are many examples in which competing rights may be advanced. For instance, the freedom to strike in pursuance of an industrial dispute may conflict with the rights of those who wish to work. In areas such as anti-discriminatory legislation, the rights of important minorities to protection may be at variance with the rights of other people to speak and act as they wish. In so many claims and counter-claims concerning social rights, the difficulty lies in balancing the desire for personal liberty and the need for measures widely perceived as being in the general good.

FREEDOM OF EXPRESSION

Freedom of expression is not viewed as an absolute right in any country, but it is a highly prized concept in many. In the First Amendment to the American Constitution, it is explicitly declared, and Article 19 of the International Covenant on Civil and Political Rights affirms the right of all people to seek, receive and impart information and ideas of all kinds, regardless of frontiers, 'either orally, in writing or in print, in the form of art, or through any other media of his choice'. Article 10 of the European Convention expresses a similar guarantee, though it does not specifically include references to seeking information and ideas.

WHY IS FREEDOM OF EXPRESSION IMPORTANT?

The right to freedom of expression is justified in several ways. Writers tend to stress the importance to a democracy of maintaining a free flow of information. In the area of political debate it is especially important, for democracy depends upon maintaining a circulation of ideas and opinions. There needs to be accessible public coverage of politicians and their policies. The Austrian Government was challenged by the European Commission on Human Rights in 1992 on account of its broadcasting provisions; it was pointed out that 'Article 10 is based on the idea that a pluralism of ideas must be safeguarded'.

Freedom of expression is important in other areas besides political discussion. People need to know about the options available to them in areas such as education, health and recreation, about how their lives may be changed as a result of present and future government plans and business practices. Although the right of free expression is actually about the supply of information, it is also important for people to be able to receive it. Granting the fullest freedom to supply is the best way of allowing people to receive.

Of course, freedom of expression is not just about informing people of choices in their political and working lives. It covers many areas from advertisements to *avant-garde* films. Artists and writers of many types use a wide variety of means to portray people's experiences and lifestyles, whether they concern personal disability or one-parent families, body-building or homosexuality. If artists and writers are allowed full freedom to discuss such themes, the ideas achieve some acceptance in popular culture: the recognition and acceptance that a group such as the gay community may get enables it to develop some sense of identity and pride in its lifestyle. By contrast, the denial of freedom of expression concerning particular actions appears to be a condemnation of the lifestyle involved. Those involved may feel that their lifestyles are being written off or devalued, and that in some way their membership of society is seen as worthless. McCrudden and Chambers refer to the importance of the Gay Pride festivals in drawing attention to the distinctive contribution to society of gays in Britain. Their actions are 'validated' in the public eye. By contrast, when the notorious Section 28 of the Local Government Act (1988) was introduced, the activities of the gay community were invalidated, for the law seemed to be an example of lifestyle censorship, implanting the thought that homosexuality was undesirable. The law prevented local authorities from promoting the teaching in schools of 'the acceptance of homosexuality as a pretended family arrangement'.

It is, then, the need to allow a circulation of ideas, and the opportunities to individuals and groups to portray lifestyles and gain recognition of their role in society, which provide the main justification for freedom of expression. For those who would limit it, the case needs to be a powerful one. The more that restrictions would lessen the transmission of knowledge and reduce the scope for validation of people's lives, the more convincing the argument needs to be. Not all materials carry the same weight, of course. In cases where accurate news reporting is involved or the public feel entitled to see government documents, the defence of free expression is especially important for prohibition would seriously limit people's chances to develop their own opinions in the light of the available evidence. On the other hand, the justification for permitting the right to fabricate sensationalist stories, to make films or display material about sado-masochism, racism or support for terrorist violence may seem relatively less fundamental.

Yet in a free society even if some issues are more intrinsically important than others, there is a need to defend all forms of expression and communication, except where those activities actually cause harm to other groups or individuals. Some are easy to justify simply because they appear to cause much good and pose little threat. However, even actions which are harmful to some individuals and groups may still be justified, and necessary as part of the price we pay for living in a free society.

Where restriction is necessary, it is important that the citizen can easily find out what the limits are so that they can adjust their behaviour accordingly. It must be demonstrated that restriction is necessary in any democratic society in that it fulfils some pressing social need, and is proportional to the aim of responding to that need. It is not enough merely to assert that some restriction is necessary for national security and public order, but to provide evidence that there is a genuine and serious danger that the state is not over-estimating, or over-reacting to.

Pluralism and tolerance are democratic virtues which suggest a maximum emphasis on freedom of expression. But there are conditions under which limitations are acceptable. Where there is a perceived and dangerous terrorist threat, there may be good grounds for restriction. Again, the European Convention and the International Covenant actually require restrictions on the advocacy of national, racial and religious hatred.

Reasons for regulation include such things as:

- national security;
- public safety – the prevention of public disorder/crime;
- protection of the rights and freedoms of others;
- public health and morals (a more controversial one).

FREEDOM OF EXPRESSION UNDER ENGLISH LAW

We have discussed the reasons why freedom of expression is commonly viewed as a basic or even a moral right. Yet in English law, such a right does not exist other than in a few specific cases. MPs may say what they want in either House of Parliament, and those who would seek to prevent them would be in contempt of Parliament. Again, the observations of judges, witnesses and jurors cannot be made the subject of civil actions. Finally, on university campuses there is something akin to a legal right to free expression, for the code of practice which Further and Higher institutions were forced to draw up in the Education Act (1986) laid down disciplinary procedures to be taken against staff or students who sought to limit free speech, unless the speaker was saying something prohibited by law. The policy was designed to stop students from denying a platform to speak to those whose views they disliked. There had in the 1960s and '70s been several cases in which right-wing politicians, and even university academics with unfashionable views, had been prevented from addressing audiences.

Beyond these examples **there is no clear legal presumption in favour of free expression**. However, judges have in recent years tried to establish a legal principle of free speech so that laws and other rules which inhibit free expression are interpreted as narrowly as possible. This is not a strong safeguard, however, because:

- although the principle of free speech may allow more latitude to individuals, it does not do the same for local authorities and charities;
- it is concerned with free speech alone, and not with other means of expression such as pictures, displays or gestures.

Freedom of expression has several aspects, including free speech, the freedom of the press, freedom of worship, freedom of assembly and freedom to march in procession. To each of those we must now turn in greater detail. In doing so, the broad principle to keep in mind is that the attitude of English law is that speakers and writers have no special protection to enable them to give free expression to their opinions. But there is no restriction which can interfere with this freedom, unless they overstep the bounds set by law and, in particular, by the law of defamation (see pp 19–21).

FREE SPEECH

Britain is a country where freedom of expression and particularly free speech are thought to be part of our heritage. As the poet John Betjeman put it:

Think of what our nation stands for
Books from Boots and country lanes
Free speech, free passes, class distinction
Democracy and proper drains.

In Westminster Abbey

A SPEAKER AT SPEAKERS' CORNER, HYDE PARK

The British attachment to free speech is symbolised by Speakers' Corner, Hyde Park, where on Sunday afternoons a variety of people, ranging from political extremists, representatives of minority ethnic groups and religious zealots, advocate their views to whomever will listen. Such activities showing the maximum tolerance of dissident opinions, indicate a mature democracy. The French political philosopher and satirist, Voltaire, recognised their cardinal importance when he said:

I disapprove of what you say, but I will defend to the death your right to say it.

There have, on occasions, been governments other than democratic ones which have asserted the right of free discussion, and permitted and encouraged criticism. It was Frederick the Great of Prussia who is said to have remarked that 'My people and I have an arrangement; they are to say what they like, and I am to do what I like'. Yet however liberal he may have been in the age of enlightened despots, such a reaction was untypical and was always likely to be transitory. Other enlightened despots of the eighteenth century reacted sharply to criticism of their performances and lifestyles. Moreover, even in those regimes which did concede the right, it was generally in the first place only as a response to the demands of a minority of the population. Where opinion is restricted to what the government in power allows to be expressed, then its value is strictly limited.

In the absence of any law proclaiming the right of free speech the British rely on what A.V. Dicey (see pp 27–29) labelled the three pillars of liberty. Between them, he argued that Parliament, a culture of liberty and the courts offered adequate protection, operating as they did against a background of respect for the rule of law. It was more than 100 years ago that Dicey wrote. But these protections have been seen by government, politicians and some members of the judiciary as sufficient to meet the requirements set out in various international documents for the protection of freedom of speech. Opponents suggest that the arrangements are so flexible and capable of varying interpretations that they allow too much scope for restrictive action.

TOLERANCE OF UNPOPULAR AND EXTREME OPINIONS

We have seen that the right to oppose is a fundamental one which embodies the spirit and proclaims the existence of a democratic system. Democracy thrives on freedom of discussion and in turn this requires that information and opinions can be supplied from a diversity of outlets. The difficulty is to decide just how much free speech should be tolerated, and what restrictions are reasonable and appropriate.

In a ruling in the case of James v the Commonwealth of Australia, 1936, the Privy Council observed:

Free speech does not means free speech; it means speech hedged in by all those laws against defamation, blasphemy, sedition and so forth. It means freedom governed by law...

As with other freedoms, there is no special protection enabling people to speak freely, but there are no restrictions to interfere with our rights unless we fall foul of particular laws, as set out on pp 18–22.

Protection of the individual

Restrictions on free speech may be urged when false information is being disseminated or false claims are made against individuals. Again, it is a dangerous path for it is easy for those with strong views themselves to assume that opponents are being misleading, and arguing a deliberately dishonest line. It is via the process of rebuttal and counter rebuttal that the public can reach an informed opinion. Sometimes the legal issues are difficult to distinguish, but where this can be done limitations may be acceptable. Where individuals are making baseless charges against someone they wish to discredit, it is reasonable for them to have recourse to law (defamation) to defend themselves.

The law can function as a protector of freedom of speech. It permits fair comment, but discourages the 'smearing' of one person by another. Where the law of libel is lax, political parties have been able to get away with the most unscrupulous smearing of political opponents. For instance , in the French 'Third Republic', rightwing groups used the most unscrupulous smear tactics against the Centre and Left, knowing that if they threw enough mud some would stick, however unjustified the accusations.

The right to express opinions freely in this country extends to all political groups provided that they do not specifically incite their audiences to acts of violence. Thus pro-anarchist, communist and fascist groups, and others less ideologically committed, can put forward their views. Members of some groups appear to believe that whilst they should be allowed to exercise their basic democratic rights, this freedom should be denied to others, especially if the latter can be branded as 'racists' or fascists'. Back in 1974, the National Union of Students took a decision to ban such speakers from universities, and shortly afterwards the Vice-Chairman of the Tory Monday Club had to flee from a howling mob at Oxford University. Barracking and disruption of meetings were for a while common on the campuses, and it was this which led to the formulation of the code of practice to which we have already referred above. Genuine free speech should surely allow the expression of unpopular and even very controversial opinions if they are lawful, and in a mature and stable democracy such as our own we err on the side of maximum tolerance and freedom of expression.

Protection of the state

Can tolerance be extended to groups who do not themselves believe in democratic values and would certainly not allow free expression if they were to be returned to power? The granting of democratic rights to those who would use their freedom to undermine and destroy a free society holds dangers. For instance, it is sometimes argued that if Weimar Germany had been less tolerant of the extremist views of the Nazi Party in the 1920s and early 1930s, it could have been strangled at birth before it ever gained a foothold. If this had happened then the destruction of all elements of democracy in Germany in the 1940s would have been prevented.

Reasonable and orderly criticism of the nature and form of government is natural and desirable, but the use of force, or the incitement to the use of force, by an extremist group is unlikely to be tolerated in any society. Even a convinced democrat may advocate the suppression of violent and extremist groups. A condition of democracy is mutual tolerance, not just toleration by one side, and those who do not abide by democratic values in their own behaviour have little right to expect it from others.

If a group shuns the use of force but devotes itself to propaganda and other activities to undermine the existing government, the greatest toleration is justified. The habit of repression can easily develop: the supression of critical opinions can be the slippery slope to a wider suppression of divergent views. Democracy cannot rest on a basis of repression, and only in exceptional circumstances should any views be outlawed. The question arises in relation to Sinn Fein, widely seen as the political arm of the Irish Republican Army (IRA). It favours a united Ireland, and there are many others who see such an outcome in the long term as a desirable goal. Any ban on Sinn Fein (see pp 55–56) can seem like a denial or the right to express republican views. It also carries the danger that groups which hold such views but are not associated with the IRA, will spring up under a different name and continue their activities. It is not easy nor is it desirable to limit people's right to express a legitimate view of long term policy, with the proviso that it is done peacefully.

FREEDOM OF THE PRESS AND OF THE MEDIA IN GENERAL

The existence or otherwise of a free press is widely seen as one of the main criteria of a democratic system. It has been supported by various arguments, and over many centuries. Censorship stifles the freedom of people to assess issues for themselves, for it denies them the necessary information to make up their mind. It provides the means by which they can get at the truth. As John Keane (*The Media and Democracy*) explains:

[a free press] is a guarantee of freedom from political coxcombs, Parliamentary hoodwinking and governmental slavery. It ensures good government, based on the natural rights of rational individuals'.

It also provides the means by which good decisions are likely to be arrived at, by making available to those in office comprehensive material about national and world affairs.

In the modern world, the value of the media as a counterweight to despotic and arbitrary government is much appreciated by those who are the victims of oppression. Often, they are unable to see or read about what is going on around them, but where newspapers continue to appear and broadcasters to broadcast hopes of freedom are kept alive. By such standards, there is little to fear in the British situation, and journalists of all kinds are keen to take any opportunities to put their views across.

Prior restraint

It was the Duke of Wellington who is alleged to have said 'publish and be damned'. This is the view taken by many journalists who argue the right to place their material in the public domain. They dislike any notion of prior restraint, the use of injunctions to stop information from appearing in the first place, for this restricts their freedom of expression. As the eminent eighteenth century legal expert, William Blackstone, put it in his *Commentaries*, 1765:

The liberty of the press is indeed essential to the nature of a free state; but this consists in laying no previous restraints on publication, and not in freedom from censure for criminal matters when published. Every free man has an undoubted right to lay what sentences he pleases before the public; to forbid this is to destroy the freedom of the Press, but if he publishes what is improper, mischievous or illegal, he must take the consequences of his temerity.

As we will see (pp 20–21, 55), prior restraint does not normally apply in defamation cases. As long as defendants can argue that an article will show fair comment or truth of observation, no injunction is granted against them. But in other matters such as cases involving a breach of confidence, injunctions against the media are granted if the commercial interest of the plaintiff appears to be more important than the defendant's right of free speech. Geoffrey Robertson quotes the example of an injunction granted to the manufacturers of the pregnancy drug, Primodos, to stop the screening of a Thames Television documentary. In this case (Schering Chemicals v Falkman Ltd, 1981), many felt that the producers were bound by an obligation of confidentiality which should not be undermined, even though Lord Denning urged that 'the public interest in receiving the information about the drug Primodos and its effects far outweighs the private interest of the makers in preventing discussion of it'.

Interim injunctions

Interim injunctions may be used to limit free speech in the political sphere. In 1987 the Radio Four series on the security services, 'My Country Right or Wrong', was the subject of an interim injunction. Although it had already been advertised in the *Radio Times*, the government successfully argued – without having actually seen the programme – that it should not be shown because former members of the services may have breached confidentiality in giving their interviews. The broadcast was delayed and the BBC ordered to hand the tapes to the Attorney General who had acted on the minister's behalf. After hearing the tapes, the government discontinued the action, and broadcasters put the series out.

THE LEGAL LIMITATIONS ON FREE EXPRESSION

The restrictions placed on what may be said and written are not stringent, and do not forbid the expression of opinions critical of the Crown or of the government of the day. Anarchist, communist or fascist speakers are all free to express their viewpoint subject only to not inciting people to acts of violence or to racial hatred.

The main constraints are as follows.

- The law of sedition
- The law of blasphemy
- The law of defamation
- Race relations legislation

THE LAW OF SEDITION

The definition of seditious libel was originally far-reaching, involving any attempt to promote ill-feeling or dissent. The law was at one time used to stifle debate involving any criticism of government policy, but the modern interpretation is much narrower. In 1909, Justice Coleridge (the King v Aldred) defined it as:

[language] intended to incite others to public disorder, to wit, rebellions, insurrections, assassinations, outrages or any physical force or violence of any kind'.

Since then, there have been relatively few prosecutions, and they have been limited to cases where the speaker or writer intended to promote violence or public disorder.

THE LAW OF BLASPHEMY

In bygone days, any attack on Christianity was thought to be blasphemous, for it exposed the faith to 'vilification, ridicule or indecency'. In the twentieth century, blasphemy has been interpreted much more narrowly, and is therefore an uncommon offence. It was, however, successfully invoked in a much publicised private prosecution against the then editor of *Gay News*, Derek Lemon (Whitehouse v Lemon, 1978). The previous year he had published a poem, 'The Love that Dares to Speak its Name', and an accompanying drawing which were held by the complainant 'to vilify Christ in His Life and His Crucifixion'. The judgement suggested that 'anything concerning God, Christ or the Christian religion' is covered, if it is written 'in terms so scurrilous, abusive or offensive as to outrage the feelings of any member or sympathiser with the Christian religion'.

The offence remains in place in spite of attempts either to widen the protection or get rid of the concept. In the Salman Rushdie case, Muslims made an unsuccessful attempt in 1990 to persuade the Divisional Court that blasphemy should be extended to protect religions other than Christianity, such as Islam. Government ministers including the Prime Minister were unwilling to contemplate any extension of blasphemy to cover other creeds, for they felt that such legislation would infringe Rushdie's freedom of expression – and that of anyone else so caught by a strengthened law.

A few years earlier, in 1985, the Law Commission had recommended that the offence of blasphemy should be removed from the statute book, but this has still not happened. Given the way in which it discriminates between the different religions and their adherents and that it does not deal with any pressing social demand, the case for removal appears to be strong.

At some time in the future, it is unlikely to withstand detailed scrutiny should a case be brought before the European Court, for the law fails to comply with accepted international standards. As Lord Denning put it as far back as 1949:

> *The reason for this law was because it was thought that a denial of Christianity was liable to shake the fabric of society, which was itself founded on the Christian religion. There is no such danger to society now'.*

THE LAW OF DEFAMATION

The law of defamation is technically divided into **slander** (defamation by word or gesture and therefore a temporary attack), and **libel** (defamation by printed word or in broadcast form, and because it is recorded a permanent form). Defamation of character is invariably a civil offence, though the arcane offence of criminal libel based on a law of 1275 still exists; in other words, a seditious comment may be a criminal offence.

The basic idea of defamation is that any statement which is calculated to bring a person into hatred, ridicule or contempt, or which may cause a person to be ostracised, is actionable in the courts, because such comment lowers the reputation of that person in the estimation of right-thinking members of society generally – a principle established in the case of Sim v Stetch, 1936. Vulgar abuse is unlikely to influence right-thinking people and is therefore unlikely to be the cause of court action, but even where the attack is more serious there may be grounds for allowing the maximum free speech. If the observation can be proved true or come into the category of fair comment, there is no legal liability.

In spite of the difficulties involved in bringing any case of defamation to court, this law remains as one of the strongest restraints on freedom of speech. Originally it was conceived as a means of stifling dissent in the French Revolution. Today, even if a person is acting in good faith or making apparently harmless statements, they can be adjudged to be defamatory by innuendo. British law is harsh in such cases, and it is up to the defendant to establish one of the defences above. Fair comment is usually interpreted sufficiently broadly to ensure that the restrictions to free speech are limited, but truth may be more difficult to establish for it requires the assemblage of sufficient admissible evidence to persuade a jury. This is a difficulty for it takes time, resources and money to prove (actions for defamation involve no legal aid on either side, and are expensive). The honour of the plaintiff is presumed in court actions, and it is up to the defendant to prove that the person suing is not of good reputation.

The risk taken by the would-be defamer is considerable. Some individuals have been only too willing to threaten court action for defamation, the late press tycoon, Robert Maxwell, being notorious for the threats he issued. Any newspaper or broadcaster therefore has to think carefully before allowing a possible defamatory story to be run, for the outcome could prove seriously damaging to their financial viability. Judges have been severe in their dealings with those found guilty of defamation. The highest award against a private individual was that made against Nikolai Tolstoy. Tolstoy had made and frequently repeated the damning claim that a high-ranking British officer, Lord Aldington, had been responsible for the forcible repatriation of Cossack and Yugoslav refugees at the end of the Second World War. By handing over 70,000 such people to the Soviet authorities, the officer was in effect a war criminal, for he knew that they would meet a cruel fate. The allegation led to him having to pay Lord Aldington £1.5 million in damages!

Klug, Starmer and Weir stress that the 'rigidity' of the defamation law runs contrary to the trend in international law which has placed greater emphasis on the right to free expression. Lord Diplock gave a similar opinion in 1980 (Gleaves v Deakin), and observed that the law was 'difficult to reconcile with international obligations which this country has undertaken by becoming a party to the European Convention'. It is true that under the terms of the European

Convention, the Court normally considers that defamation has not occurred provided that the facts are reasonably accurate, that the view was expressed in good faith and that there was no intent to defame. This being the case, there is a substantial difference between the practice of Britain and many other countries. Indeed, in a judgement in 1995, the Court accepted that the state of British law and the size of the damages awarded, were an infringement of Tolstoy's right to freedom of expression under Article 10 of the European Convention (Tolstoy Miloslavsky v UK, 1995).

RACE RELATIONS LEGISLATION

Under the 1965 and 1968 Race Relations Acts, it was made an offence to publicise views which were likely or were intended to have the effect of provoking racial disharmony. This includes the use of abuse, insulting words or behaviour likely to inflame ill-feeling. By the 1976 statute, the prosecution does not any longer have to prove an intention to incite racial hatred, only that this was the consequence of what was said or done. A further change in the wording of the law occurred in the Public Order Act (1986), so that a person can now be convicted because of the intention or the likelihood of stirring up racial hatred. this extends to the use of threatening language, the publication of insulting or abusive material, and to the possession of racially inflammatory material such as videos or literature.

For all of the strengthening of the law over the past generation, it remains the case that prosecutions are rare. There were only 20 or so in the five years after the last Race Relations Act, and since then they have been infrequent, for they require the approval of the Attorney-General and this has not often been forthcoming. Judges too have often erred on the side of free speech, as in the 1976 case involving a National Front spokesman accused of making derogatory remarks about coloured people whom he described as 'racial inferiors'. Mr Justice McKinnon waxed lyrical about the traditional rights of an Englishman to free speech, and actually wished the acquitted defendant well in his future pronouncements.

The aim of the legislation has always been to maintain civil harmony and public order rather than to curtail the expression of offensive views. The emphasis of the legislation has been less concerned with the prosecution of racist speakers and more about racial harassment. This is in line with international comparisons, for it seeks to protect minorities from the threat of violence.

Additional Limitations Affecting the Press
These limitations discussed above apply equally to the press, using the term to cover printed material of all types. In addition journalists have to be wary not to offend against the **Official Secrets Act (1989)**. The powers under the revised legislation may have been narrowed, but in key areas they are formidable,

especially concerning the right of search and seizure of material. In the prolonged *Spycatcher* case some papers were limited as to what they could publish by a court injunction (see p 55). A further limitation is the **'D' Notice** system of warning newspapers against publication of certain types of material. Journalists are expected not to report items which are believed to be injurious to the national interest.

Journalists may also fall foul of the law by committing a **contempt of court**, by publishing comments, in the course of a trial, which might make it more difficult for justice to prevail. Similarly, early disclosure of reports by Parliamentary committees could be a **contempt of Parliament**.

The **Obscene Publications Act (1959)** is another pitfall for journalists. The statute which still prevails maintained the previous definition of 'anything liable to deprave and corrupt' as a test for obscenity. Its key change was that the effect of publication taken as a whole on its likely readership was to be considered, and balanced against consideration of a new 'public good' definition which might result from publication. The new definition meant that experts could be summoned to identify literary, scientific or other merit in any work, and their insights could be assessed along with the views of the prosecution.

Many of the offences brought within the Act are in the 'dirty book' category, though occasionally a work of alleged literary merit can become the centrepiece of a spectacular case. The trial concerned with D.H. Lawrence's *Lady Chatterley's Lover* was the first major test of the 1959 Act, and the publishers (Penguin) were acquitted after a succession of eminent witnesses had given their verdict on the book.

The broad approach of English law to freedom of expression is that a speaker or writer has neither special protection nor restriction as long as the bounds set by law, and in particular by the law of defamation, are respected. The law throws the risk on the speaker, writer and publisher.

Of course, as the judge made clear in McAra v Magistrates of Edinburgh in 1913:

---

the right of free speech is a perfectly separate thing from the question of the place where it is to be exercised.

Clearly, the exercise of the former depends upon a public place being available.

THE FREEDOMS OF ASSOCIATION AND ASSEMBLY

Freedom of association involves the right of people to combine freely, without fear of arbitrary interference. It is the basis of the right of people to join a political party, a pressure group or a trade union, and to publicise their common concerns. As such, it is fundamental to any democracy that there should be the maximum entitlement to free association and assembly, for this is how a society can ensure that its members have a chance to participate fully in civil life.

Again, as we have seen in other areas involving freedom of expression, there is no positive right enabling people to associate. They need to ensure that their activities are not forbidden, and if they are not then they can express themselves in any lawful gathering. The law of conspiracy, part of the Criminal Law Act (1977), prevents anyone from joining together for the purpose of committing crime, outraging decency or corrupting public morals, and there are civil actions which can derive from two or more people agreeing to act in an unlawful manner.

The British position of allowing maximum freedom of association is in line with international obligations. There is provision under the Prevention of Terrorism Act to ban certain bodies throughout Britain, and it is illegal for people to seek to become a member of them. Such proscribed organisations are few in number, and currently only the IRA and the Irish National Liberation Army (INLA) are outlawed. It is an offence for anyone to address a meeting of three or more people in support of either of these bodies. In Northern Ireland, the control is more severe, and the Emergency Provisions Act (1991) allows for more proscription – hence the ban on the Ulster Defence Association and the Ulster Volunteer Force in the province.

The civil position is less clear-cut. For instance, in the protest at Twyford Down in the early 1990s, peaceful motorway protesters were categorised in the same way as those among them who committed damage to vehicles used by building firms. All were restrained by an injunction from further protest, and made to pay a proportion of Department of Transport costs.

Labour relations are an important aspect of rights of freedom of association. The right to join a trade union (or not to join one), and to pursue labour objectives through collective action is one acknowledged in the Universal Declaration of Human Rights. It is well-established in international law, and the UN Covenant and European Convention explicitly recognise it. As with other forms of freedom of association, the right can be limited, but only is this is necessary for the preservation of a democratic society. Since the early nineteenth century, Britain has allowed trade unions legally to exist, and the right to membership has been more recently guaranteed under the 1992 Trade Union and Labour Relations Act. However, the decision of the Thatcher government to ban civil servants at Government Communications Headquarters (GCHQ) from joining trade unions was a controversial one. In this case, security considerations led to the action, and these were upheld by the House of Lords, the International Labour Organisation (ILO) and the European Commission, although they greatly antagonised members of the Trades Union Congress (TUC) and many others in and out of the Labour movement. The 1997 Labour government subsequently lifted the prohibition.

Allied to freedom of association is **freedom of assembly**, a right which is exercised every time young people visit the pub or the cinema. More controversial are those occasions on which they meet in rallies and festivals, for purposes of political discussion or protest. People may come together in a public meeting provided that they can hire premises or meet on private property. To use a public facility, such as a park or shopping centre, they need permission. There is no general right to stage a gathering in Trafalgar Square, even though it has often been seen as a haven for those who wish to register their disapproval of government policy. Such a gathering actually requires the permission of the relevant Secretary of State, under the terms of the regulations about the Square laid down in 1952. In general terms, at any meeting people may say what they wish provided that it does not either render likely or cause a breakdown in public order.

Such meetings are a vital part of life in any democratic country, and the right to express political discontent in marches and demonstrations allows 'people power' to find an outlet, providing an opportunity for views to be put forward, often of a kind which do not get much coverage in the media or via other institutions such as Parliament. Hence the observation of a representative for the UN Centre for Human Rights in 1994:

The right of assembly must be respected, since public demonstrations and political rallies are an integral part of the election process and provide an effective mechanism for the public dissemination of political information.

PROCESSIONS AND PROTEST MARCHES

It is traditional for British people to wish to demonstrate their feelings on a political issue via a **procession or protest march**; in so doing they are behaving lawfully if they are not breaking a particular law. There are limitations on where they can exercise this freedom, however. They may do so on the public highway as long as they keep moving, and act in an orderly manner. If they stop, they may be guilty of obstruction under the Highways Act (1980), for roads are designed for the movement of traffic from one place to another. They may also be causing a public nuisance. The issue of demonstrating along the highways may seem relatively unimportant, at most an inconvenience, but during the Miners' Strike of 1984 the courts found that 'unreasonable harassment' of workers seeking to get to their place of employment was a form of 'nuisance' which was unacceptable.

More threatening to society is a situation in which extreme political activists wish to march. The Public Order Act (1936) was designed to deal with the rise of Sir Oswald Mosley's pro-fascist 'blackshirts' in the 1930s. It gave the police the right to change the route of a proposed march, and to impose conditions on the way it was organised. In particular, the carrying of weapons or wearing of uniforms, were banned. Today, the same issues arise. The freedom of the National Front to hold a rally may well conflict with the rights of local residents who do not wish to have provocative marchers passing near to their door; here the right to carry out an activity has to be balanced against the concerns of other citizens. The issue arises most dramatically in Northern Ireland, for in the 'marching season' supporters of either side claim their right to celebrate their past history by parading with banners – often along 'sensitive' areas populated by their religious opponents.

In Britain, the law has been updated in recent years, because of the number of rallies which have led to some measure of violence. The Public Order Act (1986) removed some offences present under the old law, and created new ones. As we have seen, the law on racial hatred was clarified and tightened, and the law on riot, violent disorder and affray has been amended. Riot is the most serious offence under the Act, for it carries a penalty of up to ten years imprisonment. A riot involves the activities of 12 or more persons who use, or threaten to use, unlawful violence.

The right to assemble and protest is not guaranteed by law in Britain, but in the European Convention and the International Covenant this is seen as a key element in a democratic society. There the freedom is proclaimed, and the exceptions then follow. In Britain, the negative freedom to meet and protest exists, but it is hemmed in with a series of restrictions. In their democratic audit, Klug, Starmer and Weir echo the feelings of many other writers that in the balancing of the rights of individuals and groups on the one hand to protest and on the other hand to enjoy order and safety, it is the latter which get the greater emphasis. They conclude that:

> *In the United Kingdom, freedom of assembly – and protest – is increasingly permitted only when the cost to public convenience is low and the protest does not arouse official disapproval or distaste.*

FREEDOM OF RELIGION AND CONSCIENCE

Associated with freedom of expression and association is freedom of religion and the right to worship or not to do so. Any religion or cult has the right to hold a service and practise its rituals, although there have been occasions when the definition of a religion or the nature of a group's behaviour have caused problems. Scientologists claim to be a religion, and deny that their behaviour is harmful or exploitative, but in Britain and elsewhere their status has been a cause of controversy.

BRITAIN'S EXAMPLE IN THE PROTECTION OF RIGHTS

In Britain, there has long been pride in the commitment to liberty, and the Westminster model of democracy was for many years admired by politicians and constitutional experts in many countries. They looked to it for inspiration, and in planning their own governmental arrangements they were keen to enlist the assistance of those well-versed in British practice. As Ewing and Gearty observe:

If a country enacted a bill of rights, then it was likely to be acknowledged as a written but inadequate consolation for the absence of that commitment to liberty which appeared to seep unconsciously and effortlessly through the British system of government.

When the Attlee Governments of 1945–51 were involved in the drafting and promotion of the European Convention of Human Rights (ECHR), there was little thought that it was necessary for the guarantees it provided to be written into British law, for it was recognised that the British arrangements were superior to those elsewhere in the world. This is not true today, and whilst in Britain there is now growing anxiety about the vulnerability of traditional freedoms it is other countries which have led the way in devising new and more effective instruments for the protection of rights.

THE BRITISH APPROACH

In Britain, we have a negative approach to rights. Few of them are guaranteed by law so that we can do or say something provided that there is no law against it. Unlike the situation in other western democracies, there is no bill of rights or document setting out our basic entitlements. This is at variance with the approach adopted by the European Convention on Human Rights (see Chapter 4), which, for instance, proclaims the right of assembly, and then makes exceptions to it.

No restrictions shall be placed on the exercise of these rights other than such as are prescribed by law and are necessary in a democratic society in the interests of national security or public safety, for the prevention of disorder or crime, for the protection of health or morals or for the protection of the rights and freedoms of others.

British law does not make assembly a positive right, but we are free to assemble to the extent that we are not restricted by a law, whether statute or judge-made. Thus the constitutional expert of the late nineteenth century, A.V. Dicey, could observe that the 'right of assembling is nothing more than a result of the view taken by the courts as to individual liberty of the person and individual liberty of speech'. He nonetheless believed that the British approach provided a more certain basis for protecting freedom than did the more positive and sweeping declarations often included in constitutions elsewhere.

Many of our rights have evolved and been recognised over many centuries, and are now seen as traditional ones. We have primarily relied upon custom and the ordinary law of the land (the common law and specific statutes) for our protection, secure in the knowledge that the individual has the ultimate right of redress in the courts if an injustice has been done.

THE VIEWS OF A.V. DICEY

When **A.V. Dicey** wrote his *Introduction to the Study of the Law of the Constitution* in 1885, he identified the three pillars of liberty and the rule of law as our best protection. The pillars were Parliament, public opinion and the courts. The good sense and vigilance of Members of Parliament, the 'culture of liberty' shared by the British people, and the justice available to individuals via the judicial system were seen as notable safeguards in themselves. Above all, there was the commitment to the rule of law. For Dicey, the concept involved three main propositions:

1 That 'no man [was] punishable or [could] be made to suffer in body or goods except for a distinct breach of law established in the ordinary legal manner before the ordinary courts in the land'.
2 The assumption 'not only that no man [was] above the law, but that here every man, whatever be his rank or condition, [was] subject to the ordinary law of the realm and amenable to the jurisdiction of the ordinary tribunals'.
3 That 'the general principles of the Constitution (as for example the right to personal liberty, or the right of public meeting) are with us as the result of judicial decisions determining the rights of private persons in particular cases brought before the courts'.

In his writings on the Constitution, the implications of the rule of law for individual liberty were made clearly apparent. 'The right to personal freedom' was guaranteed by 'the strict maintenance of the principle that no man [could] be arrested or imprisoned, except in due course of law...under some warrant or authority'. Similarly with 'freedom of expression; 'Any man may...say or write whatever he likes, subject to the risk of, it may be, severe punishment if he publishes any statement (either by word of mouth, in writing or in print) which he is not legally entitled to make'. With freedom of assembly, the treatment again follows the same pattern; 'It can hardly be said that our Constitution knows of such a thing as any specific right of public meeting'.

He approved of the 'absence of those declarations or definitions of rights so dear to foreign constitutionalists', for he saw it as a strength that the emphasis on specific remedies protected by legislation and the courts could only be overturned by 'nothing less than a revolution'. By contrast, 'general rights guaranteed by the constitution may be, and in foreign countries, constantly are, suspended'.

Dicey's ideas have long held currency in the British debate on rights, and those who oppose any move towards a bill of rights are often heard to proclaim that the existence of our liberties rests on firmer foundations than any listing of personal rights. The rights of Englishmen rest on our traditions, our respect for the rule of law, and our free Parliament, concepts and institutions which have survived for hundreds of years unlike the often short-lived continental experience of constitutions where – given an invasion, a war or a coup – the whole system can be thrown into turmoil.

This is a negative defence of rights, but Dicey was sure that even allowing for the specific restraints on freedom there was still plenty of scope for the individual to have his rights. Parliament and the courts would ensure that those rights were upheld. But what if it is actually Parliament, at the behest of the executive which commands a majority of support in the House, which is producing new and restrictive laws?

A study of the first 37 violations of the European Convention (1959–95) by Klug, Starmer and Weir reveals that 24 were the work of Parliament, including legislation on closed shops, corporal punishment, prisoners' rights and many other topics. The House of Commons often fails to check legislation which breaches the European document. It is little consolation to be told by the Conservative MP Bill Walker, in a House of Commons debate (1993), that 'citizens rights are protected by the fact that Parliament is not bound by decisions made by previous Parliaments. If we get something wrong, as we often do, we can rectify it the following year'.

Ewing and Gearty too are doubtful of the protection offered by Dicey's pillars, and point to a narrowing of the area of freedom;

[In Dicey's view] Freedom is not something that can be asserted in opposition to law; it is the residue of conduct permitted in the sense that no statute or common-law rule prohibits it. Undoubtedly there was such a reservoir of unregulated behaviour in Dicey's day...The residue of liberty just gets smaller and smaller, until eventually, in some areas, it is extinguished altogether, with freedom becoming no more than the power to do that which an official has

> *decided for the time being not to prohibit. The British approach of refusing to assert positive rights gives freedom no weapons with which to retaliate...Freedom retreats in the face of laws that are constantly emerging, evolving, and accumulating – but very rarely disappearing. They originate not only in Parliament but also in the courts.*

Dicey seemed to feel sure that individual liberty would be soundly supported by British judges whose commitment to freedom would be the protection from despotism. Some judges have a creditable record of protecting liberty, and have gone out of their way – via their judgements and in public speeches and articles – to uphold the traditional rights of British citizens. Critics, as we shall see later (see pp 99, 103), have less confidence in many of them, and believe that with their untypical social background, the emphasis of their legal training and their natural support for order, they are not able or willing to uphold the rights of ordinary people, let alone those of unpopular minorities. Ewing and Gearty particularly mention the way in which judges invented new laws over the Miners' Strike in 1984, or rediscovered old ones to curb the rights of demonstrators to exercise their right of peaceful assembly. There are too many examples, ranging from the *Spycatcher* case to the Ponting one (see pp 53–55), in which the courts have seen their task as to identify the interests of the state with those of the government of the day. During the *Spycatcher* saga, as the government sought to ban publication, no one could be certain which law the courts would discover in their determination to stop reports from being produced. In the areas of civil liberties, the courts seem to have come to regard themselves as the partners of the executive, tackling difficult problems together, rather than as a separate, autonomous and sometimes necessarily antagonistic branch of government. This is a long way from Dicey's reliance on them as the guardians of British rights.

SECURING RIGHTS

We have already referred to some of the ways in which an individual can protect himself and gain redress, and some writers and politicians believe that there are sufficient means within our political system to make further action unnecessary. There are legal safeguards through the courts of law and other non-legal ones which offer protection. The pamphlet *Human Rights in the United Kingdom* (COI) draws attention to some of these. There are vital non-legal safeguards against the abuse of governmental power; these include unwritten Parliamentary conventions, the sense of 'fair play' of legislators and administrations, the vigilance of the Parliamentary opposition parties and of individual MPs, the influence of a free press and public opinion, and the right to change the government through free elections with a secret ballot.

The key questions are:

● Are these non-legal means of protection adequate?

● Can we rely on Parliament to protect us?

The problem usually identified is the rise in the power of the executive branch of government. We have a situation in which executive proposals are supported by a strong system of party discipline in the House which ensures that almost any bill can be carried by a government with a clear majority. Often there is insufficient consultation, scrutiny and debate, and bills can be pushed through which deny fundamental rights.

This is indeed the problem, that Parliament which is traditionally seen as the defender of individual rights is so dominated by the executive that it can push through legislation which removes those rights. If it seems to exist to do the government's bidding, it is not surprising that individual liberty should become a casualty of the trends in the system of government.

How effectively does Parliament defend civil liberties?

The concept of Parliamentary sovereignty is a fundamental feature of the British Constitution, and it is Parliament – as the supreme legislative body – which has the power to make and unmake laws. It is the elected chamber, the House of Commons, which has the lead role, and over a long period it has been commonplace for academic and other commentators to talk of the 'passing' of Parliament and to lament the lack of effective Parliamentary control. The growth of party discipline, and of the amount and complexity of bills passed by modern governments, are often blamed for this deficiency.

In practice, it is the government which runs Parliament rather than Parliament which controls the government. Our electoral system tends to produce majority administrations and this feature and the tight party discipline which normally prevails combine to make any government potentially strong, stable and effective. For critics of Parliament's role in protecting freedoms, it is this government dominance which is at the root of the problem. Ewing and Gearty note that ministers backed by less than half of the voting public but with a Parliamentary majority can introduce legislation which is highly damaging to individual rights.

Examples of a government using its majority to hurry through 'draconian' legislation are plentiful. In particular, the Commonwealth Immigrants Act (1968) passed through all of its Parliamentary stages within a week, and the prevention of Terrorism Act did so in less than 48 hours. Other measures detrimental to individual rights such as the Criminal Justice and Public Order Act (1994) have been through the Parliamentary process. Indeed, in many of the cases in which Britain has been found guilty in the Court of Human Rights, it is Parliamentary legislation which is the cause of the difficulty, which casts doubt on the usefulness of Parliament as the defender of individual liberty.

Moreover, if Parliament had been effective in this area, it would have been unnecessary for so many cases to have been fought – often successfully – in the Commission and Court. It is significant that in many bills which come before the House of Commons there is very little mention of whether or not the measure meets the criteria of the European Convention, suggesting that many MPs as well as ministers are unaware of – or indifferent to – its requirements. When violations have been found to occur, in several cases the resulting legislation to amend the position of British law has been the minimum necessary to ensure sufficient compliance.

HOW PARLIAMENT CAN HELP INDIVIDUALS AND DISADVANTAGED GROUPS

If many people find ample evidence to doubt Parliament's capacity to defend civil liberties, others might point to ways in which it has acted on behalf of the individual. Some MPs are vigilant and effective in pursuing individual grievances against those in authority, and especially if they are on the government side they may be able to influence ministers to safeguard rights. Their influence will be all the greater if the cause they espouse represents a concern of a sizeable body of voters, if it is backed by other MPs and if the government lacks a healthy majority. Some MPs are strong defenders of civil liberties, and have spoken up for the rights of prisoners, women and many others in Parliamentary debates.

In addition, MPs can initiate private members' bills, and successful legislation of this type has promoted changes affecting the rights of consenting adults, those seeking an abortion, and those who would have been subject to capital punishment. (NB Not all of legislation based on free votes in the House has shown a respect for minority rights. The age of consent for gay young men – fixed at 18 in 1994 – is viewed by many libertarian activists as an infringement of natural justice, the more so as it conflicts with the age at which heterosexual sex is legally permitted.)

Parliament can defend civil rights in other ways. Via its select committees, there can be pressure to widen rights for various groups in the community; for instance, the Home Affairs Committee has in the 1980s argued for more sanitary prison conditions. Parliament has passed important anti-discriminatory legislation in several areas. This actually confers positive rights, most recently affecting the position of the disabled. The Equal Pay Act (1970) sought to remove the unfairness of women receiving unequal wages for equal work, and the Sex Discrimination Act (1975) and the Race Relations Act (1976) (following two earlier ones in 1965 and 1968) have both sought to improve the rights of disadvantaged groups and afford them greater protection. In both cases, however, the safeguards fall short of those undertaken in our international obligations under the International Covenant (Article 2) and the European Convention (Article 14).

To assume that Parliament alone can be relied upon to provide sufficient protection for rights would perhaps be naive. In various ways it can help individuals and groups to secure rights, but many writers feel that reliance upon the good sense of ministers and other elected politicians provides only a fragile basis for securing our essential liberties.

NB For more information on the protection offered by judges and the courts in the area of civil liberties, see pp 122–23.

SECURING RIGHTS; A SUMMARY OF THE MEANS AVAILABLE

There are several ways in which an individual may seek a remedy for wrongs done, the approach varying according to the particular case. If property rights have been ignored or overridden, as in the Crichel Down case after the war, there may have been maladministration. Since 1967, any 'injustice arising from maladministration' can be taken to the **Parliamentary Commissioner for Administration**. If a department's use of its discretionary powers has been involved, then an appeal to the appropriate tribunal may be the best way forward.

In cases involving civil rights, the aggrieved individual may:

- write to the newspapers;
- seek the attention of the **media**;
- **lobby an MP**;
- work through a **pressure group** such as Liberty;
- or engage in demonstrations and other forms of **direct action**.

Some **MPs** are very effective in taking up individual grievances, and exploiting opportunities in the House and in the media to advance their case.

In many cases, individuals and groups have gone to **court** to gain redress, but this can be a daunting and costly process, and still may not yield the required outcome.

What else can be done, once the appeals built into the legal system have been utilised?

In recent years, the **European solution** has been increasingly used. In some cases, an answer can be reached via the machinery of the **European Union**. EU law embodies much of the spirit of the European Convention, and the decisions of the European Court of Justice in Luxembourg have sometimes brought advantages to British citizens. Women have particularly benefited from decisions involving rights at the workplace.

A direct approach to the Luxembourg Court is most unusual, and is very costly. More common is an approach either to the European Commission or to the European Parliament. Petitions submitted have included ones on pension entitlements, social security benefits and the treatment of the sexes, among a range of other things. For people who travel extensively in the Union, recourse to the European machinery can be especially helpful. It was as a result of EC judgements (this was before the European Community became a Union), that Jackie Drake gained an Invalid Care Allowance previously only available to men and single women. Helen Marshall, a dietician in the NHS, won a right to work on until the age of 65, just as men normally did.

The other European solution involves an approach to the machinery of the **European Convention**, which is covered in detail on pp 78, 81–4. Such a case may go to the Strasbourg Court which should not be confused with the Luxembourg one which is part of the EU machinery.

The European dimension, whether it be an approach to the EU or to Strasbourg, is one of growing importance. It is available to British citizens, but it is not the way to achieve speedy justice. It may well work and a number of citizens have gained the outcome they were looking for, but many commentators, be they journalists, lawyers or politicians, feel that a more certain basis for the protection of our freedoms is required.

THE EFFECTIVENESS OF BRITISH PROTECTION

The arrangements for remedying infringements of individual liberty currently fall, then, into those which are purely domestic ones, and those which derive from British membership of European and international systems for protecting rights. As Klug, Starmer and Weir point out, there is a curious duality about the British position:

> *Aggrieved citizens may first of all seek to secure their rights in domestic courts, which follow a 'non-positive' approach; and if unsatisfied, may take the 'positive' road to the European Commission and Court in Strasbourg.*

The Court regularly finds that there has been some violation of the Convention, and the British Government is then obliged to change the law. But it does so only by removing the specific cause of offence. It does not proceed to offer a new positive right. Hence the comment of the UN Human Rights Committee in 1995, that the system for protecting and securing political and civil rights in the UK 'does not ensure fully that an effective remedy is provided for all violations of the rights contained in the Covenant'.

Any democratic system can devise a means of protecting rights, and the approach does not have to be a positive one to be successful. Neither the International Covenant nor the European Convention lays down a particular system as necessary, only that whichever method is adopted the outcome should be that there is an effective degree of protection. Positive systems are not inherently superior to negative ones, and even a positive document such as the Convention is capable of being developed and improved by consenting states who can add on their own extra layers of protection.

Britain has not gone down that route. British citizens have never had any form of written pact with their governments which clearly defined the limits of state power. Magna Carta stated a compromise reached between the King and barons, but this was a deal on the extent of aristocratic privileges rather than on citizens' rights. The Bill of Rights (1688), in spite of its name, was essentially a settlement of the position and rights of Parliament in relating to the Sovereign. A succession of reform movements achieved significant political advances, such as the right to vote and to combine in furtherance of workers' rights. But as Geoffrey Robertson has pointed out, the advances were about who should exercise power rather than how it is exercised:

British history has bequeathed no statute of liberty, no bill of rights forged on the anvil of revolution, to serves either as a check on overweening authority or as a checklist against which to measure the standards of justice achieved by legislation and legal decisions. Remarkably, a language rich in the rhetoric of liberty has never been deployed to enumerate, in an authoritative and binding code, the contents of the 'rights' with which those who speak it shall possess.

THE BRITISH RECORD ON RIGHTS; SOME INTERNATIONAL COMPARISONS

British Governments of recent years have taken the view that all is well with the protection of rights in Britain. Under Labour as well as the Conservatives, it has been stated in successive reports to the UN Human Rights Committee that Britain is meeting the standards laid down by the Covenant (1977, 1984, 1989 and 1994).

Some other findings have broadly endorsed this outlook. In its *World Human Rights Guide, The Economist* analysed the record of 120 countries, to assess their human rights performance. Using a questionnaire of 40 questions based upon articles of UN treaties, it concluded that the UK had a rating of 94%, a performance only bettered in Switzerland, West Germany (as it then was), the four countries of Scandinavia and New Zealand. Overall, the UK received a definite 'yes' on 33 questions, and a qualified 'yes' on the other seven. Noting that the individual was generally respected, the government was answerable to the people, that there existed a free press and balanced broadcasting, it praised the liberal democratic traditions. It mentioned that the lack of a written constitution meant that there was no formal guarantee of rights, and pointed to only a very few areas of concern – the extension of police powers, 'the major human rights problems of Northern Ireland' and the potential for social division brought about by class division, high unemployment and racial tension.

There have been other attempts to monitor human rights performances which use a similar 'quantitative' approach, based upon data received in answer to questions. They are open to doubt, for they do not distinguish between different types of violation. The US gets the best score in the world on support for political rights and civil liberties, but there is no attempt to distinguish between the fine record on open government and the less solid one on conditions in prisons; the length of detention for prisoners on death row may be seen as a serious blot on the US landscape. In Britain, the generally good record on stop and search powers used by the police conceals the fact that young people, especially Afro-Asians, are disproportionately likely to be victims of such treatment.

SOME PROBLEMS HIGHLIGHTED

The democratic audit

Klug, Starmer and Weir sought to examine the protection of democratic rights in Britain, to see how effective the remedies were for citizens whose rights have been violated. To do so, they devised a Human Rights Index which involved a qualitative and a quantitative approach. Their criteria were based upon instruments such as the International Covenant and the European Convention, and on the interpretations given to them by supervisory bodies such as the UN Human Rights Committee, the European Commission and the European Court. The comments, decisions and judgements of such bodies which monitor and in some cases enforce the documents, are the 'performance indicators'. The 'test' on any given civil and political right involved three parts;

1 Any restriction must be 'prescribed by law'.
2 The restriction must be justified by one of the aims recognised under the Covenant or Convention.
3 The restriction must be shown to be 'necessary in a democratic society'.

The findings of their audit, the first thorough analysis of British compliance with international human rights standards, provide a snapshot of standards in 1995. Published in 1996, they made for much less complacent reading. Their research covered the postwar era with particular reference to the period 1975–95, and represented an attempt to establish a clear picture of the state of political rights and freedoms. It found 42 violations and 22 near-violations, or causes for anxiety.

The writers concluded that:

> *the United Kingdom offers far less formal legal protection of fundamental political rights and freedoms than international standards require and ordinary citizens are entitled to expect.*

Breaches of the standards occurred across the whole spectrum of issues examined, and they were not odd statutes which were too narrowly drawn or protections which were patchy in their operation. Rather, they detected a 'weakness at the very heart of Britain's political and constitutional system'. They acknowledged the importance of the European and international dimension, but were perturbed that although the British courts could bear in mind such external instruments they rarely do so. They could find only ten cases since the 1970s in which the International Covenant has been alluded to in the higher courts, and only 173 involving the European Convention.

Because the courts have generally been unwilling to introduce such international procedures into the British judicial process, they see the case for incorporation as a strong one – for this would provide an effective domestic remedy when rights are violated. But they make the point that there are other ways in which rights could be protected. It would be possible to conduct a review of all laws and practices to see if they meet international obligations, a suitable task for the Law Commission which examines laws with a view to recommending modernisation (removal or amendment), where necessary. New laws could be checked for compliance as they are drawn up.

They see merit in the outcome of the journey to Strasbourg, even if this should not, in their view, be necessary. But the reluctance of governments to undertake a general view of the problem which led to the grievance is a matter for regret. Too often, the response of ministers is to deal with the specific point challenged by the applicant. Hence their lament that:

This grudging and unsystematic attitude means that the protection of political rights and freedoms in the UK generally moves forward in a slow, crab-like progression, by small increments, directed by the haphazard nature of individual applications and driven by the stick of Strasbourg. On occasion, the beast moves so slowly or reluctantly that adverse European Court judgements pile up around its unsteady advance (as, for example, in a series of prisoners' rights cases in the 1980s).

The European Convention (and similarly the Covenant) impose obligations on Britain to 'secure the rights and freedoms it contains'. What has happened is that on a series of individual cases, and in a haphazard manner, change has come about as a result of adverse verdicts. Many cases never get that far, for it may be that the aggrieved person does not pursue the case because of the money and time involved; some cases that get to Strasbourg are dealt with by the Commission; others are resolved by 'friendly settlements' and never get to court – payment of compensation can be a useful means of avoiding a damaging and embarrassing review of British practice.

The Human Rights Committee

It is not just the authors of *The Three Pillars of Liberty* who are concerned about the British record. In 1995, the UN Human Rights Committee produced its own verdict on the situation, and it also found a lack of provision for effective remedy in the British armoury. It felt that this deficiency was caused by the combined effect of:

- non-incorporation of the ECHR into British law;
- the absence of a domestic bill of rights;
- the refusal to allow individual citizens to petition the Human Rights Committee.

Among the weaknesses it discerned, special mention was given to the problems caused by racial and ethnic discrimination, the role of women in society and state practice concerning Northern Ireland. Other topics ranged from prison conditions to the lack of credibility in internal investigations by the police force.

Geoffrey Robertson and many others have concluded that the overall picture of the protection available in Britain offers no cause for complacency:

> *That most progress in the protection of civil liberties over the past decade has been directly inspired by the EU or the European Court of Human Rights in Strasbourg stands as a reproach to our own institutions, where slothfulness and secrecy, rather than any desire to oppress, have been the major obstacles to necessary reforms. Our preference for pragmatism rather than principle has been convenient in the short term; its cost may be measured in the gaps which still remaining the rights of British citizens to obtain speedy, effective or indeed any remedy against abuses of private and public power.*

CONCLUSION

In Britain, few of our rights are guaranteed by law. They are – in many cases – negative rights, which allow us to do something on the understanding that we are not violating any laws. For some people, such protection is sufficient, far superior to that provided in any single codified document. They feel that our protection derives from our tradition of liberty, and that in some way Parliament, the courts and our political culture can be relied on to look after the interests of the citizen.

Critics of the extent of state power in Britain rest their case upon the absence of guaranteed rights, the piecemeal nature of possible remedies and the evidence of numerous surveys at home and abroad which draw attention to disquieting features of the position of the individual and minority groups in our country. In the following chapter, we can examine more specifically some of the grounds for their increased concern.

Table 1: *Summary: Civil Freedoms and their protection in Britain*	
CIVIL LIBERTIES/RIGHTS	RELEVANT LEGISLATION/PROTECTION
Basic civil rights	
1 Legal rights, eg	
• freedom from police detention without charge; • right to be brought promptly to court; • presumption of innocence till guilt proved; • right to silence.	Magna Carta/Habeas Corpus both cover wrongful detention Prompt appearance covered under the Police and Criminal Evidence Act (1984), known as PACE
2 Political rights, eg • to vote at periodic elections.	Representation of People Acts, eg • 1918/28 votes for women, 1969 votes at 18
3 Freedom of expression, eg • to receive/impart information • press freedom	Limits derive from laws of blasphemy, defamation, obscenity, OSA, and 'D' Notices, race relations, sedition, etc.
4 Freedom of association/to demonstrate, eg • for social and political purposes.	No clearly defined freedom; laws of nuisance, trespass, obstruction, etc.
5 Freedom of movement, eg • to move freely around the country and leave/return.	PTA (powers of Home Secretary to detain suspected terrorists)
6 Freedom of religion/conscience, eg • to worship or not to do so; • to withhold child from attendance in RE lessons.	Some legal protection against disturbances for religious gatherings
Social Rights	
1 Employment rights	Employment Protection Act (1978) and other positive rights granted over the last generation such as those on equal pay, gender, race, etc.

2 Privacy rights, eg	
● freedom from bugging/phone tapping;	No general rights, but some specific measures such as laws on nuisance, trespass etc.
● freedom from harassment by media.	
3 Property rights, eg	Various forms of taxation, measures of compulsory purchase and nationalisation
● to own/dispose of property.	
4 Social rights eg	Specific legislation, eg 1967 acts on abortion and consenting adults
● to marry/divorce; ● to have an abortion; ● to participate in homosexual relationships.	

STUDY GUIDES

Revision Hints

You need to have a clear idea of the main rights claimed by individuals and groups, and of the differences in approach between the political Left and Right. It may be useful to draw up a table listing the main rights claimed, and any limitations on the exercise of them. Also, under the heading 'How Rights can be Enforced', list the main ways by which individuals can obtain justice. Finally, write a paragraph or two on where protection for rights comes from in Britain, in the absence of a written constitution.

If your examination board asks specific questions on press freedom or free speech, then write three paragraphs on the issue. In the first, explain the reasons for it, in the second its importance and in the third, the restrictions placed upon it in Britain today. It is useful at this stage to be familiar with one or two key areas in which freedoms are said to be under attack.

Examination Hints

Examination questions are likely to be of two main types. They may require you to comment on the effectiveness with which rights are protected in modern

Britain. Otherwise, they may relate to one particular area such as free speech or freedom of the press. A good knowledge of either area could be helpful in providing examples to show how effectively rights in Britain are secured.

As an example of a possible question, see Practice Question 5 below. Note the importance of key words 'best', 'protect' and 'promote'. You are being asked to make a judgement on the relative merits of existing avenues. Several bodies are involved, some more effective than others. Assess their usefulness. Some are more concerned to protect, than to promote.

Having defined civil liberties, you might go through those designed to protect liberties (tribunals, ombudsman MPs and Parliament, courts, judges, the media, European machinery), and comment on their strengths and limitations. Then look at those more concerned to promote, especially pressure groups such as Liberty and the Freedom Association, but also MPs, Parliament, judges etc. How do such bodies protect, and in what ways do they promote, liberties?

Your conclusion will reflect the balance of your earlier argument and examples. Ask yourself whether Parliament is as effective as Dicey assumed. Are our liberties effectively defended? Can Europe help? Do we need a bill of rights, etc.?

Group Work

There are several themes which could provide fertile ground for individual enquiry or lively class discussion. Each member could be allocated one liberty or right and be asked to survey its development in Britain, comment on its importance and the limitations upon it, and then report back to the rest of the group. This could lead into a discussion of which freedoms are the most important in Britain today. In certain areas like the Prevention of Terrorism Act, the right to abortion or the Rushdie case, there is good material for a frank exchange of views. The latter case provides an interesting example of the way in which rights may conflict, and raises the issue of whether the blasphemy laws are still appropriate in modern Britain. Depending on the composition of the group, the rights of the disabled, of ethnic minorities, gays or women to equal treatment could provoke productive controversy. How about a debate on the theme that 'This house believes that members of ethnic groups need to be accorded positive discrimination as the only means of achieving equal status'?

Practice Questions

1 What contribution is made by the law in guaranteeing minority rights to British citizens?
2 Should there be any limitations on the freedom of the individual?
3 'Freedom of expression is a defining characteristic of a democracy'. Discuss.
4 Does Britain have a free press? (You will be able to answer this more effectively if you have studied the ownership of the British press and the trend

towards a concentration of newspapers in too few hands, with a consequent narrowing in the range of opinions which can be read).

5 Which bodies best protect and promote civil liberties in Britain?

Glossary

Blackshirts Supporters of the pro-fascist leader, Oswald Mosley, in the 1930s

Blasphemy Insulting or ridiculing God or the Christian religion

Defamation An attack upon someone's good name, orally or in print

Incorporation Inclusion (eg of the European Convention into British law)

Injunction A court order to refrain from some act such as publication

Obscenity Something liable to corrupt or deprave

Official secrecy The habit of keeping information relating to government secret

OSA Official Secrets Act

Prior restraint Restraint imposed prior to a speech being made or a newspaper published

PTA Prevention of Terrorism Act

Sedition An offence which tends to undermine the authority of the state and incite a serious breach of public order

Further Reading and Resources

Amnesty International, (1997), *Fear and Silence, A Hidden Human Rights Crisis*, London

Central Office of Information (1995), *Human Rights in the United Kingdom*, London

Dicey, A. V. (1885), *Introduction to the Study of the Law of the Constitution*, Macmillan

The *Economist* (1992), *World Human Rights Guide*, UUP

Ewing and Gearty, (1990) *Freedom under Thatcher*, Clarendon Press

Keane, J. (1991), *The Media and Democracy*, Polity Press

Klug, Starmer and Weir (1996) *The Three Pillars of Liberty*, London, Routledge

Liberal Democrat Federal Green Paper 1, (1988), 'The Rights and Liberties of the Citizen'

McCrudden and Chambers (1995), *Individual Rights and the Law in Britain*, Oxford, Clarendon Press

Robertson, G. (1995), *Freedom, the individual and the Law*, London, Penguin

3

RECENT CONCERNS

Introduction

THERE ARE CONFLICTING judgements on the fate of liberties and rights in the years of Conservative rule, 1979–97. Some writers believe that this was an era in which the relationship between the individual and the state profoundly changed, in a way which was highly damaging to citizens and minority groups. Charter 88, a pressure group which advocates a bill of rights among other constitutional reforms, takes this view, and argues that 'the intensification of authoritarian rule in the United Kingdom has only recently begun'. Professor Dworkin, no admirer of the Conservative administrations, nonetheless feels that, 'the erosion of liberty is not the doing of only one party or one government'. He notes that the process predates Margaret Thatcher, and that Labour governments of the 1960s and 1970s often compromised the rights of immigrants, journalists and others.

Right-leaning academics tend to dispute the notion that the Conservatives were indifferent to liberty, and argue that in as much as there were more curbs on the freedom of the individual this was necessary to preserve society against the attack of lawbreakers and – in particular – terrorists. They also point to the increase in economic freedoms, brought about by the selling of council houses, the privatisation of state-run industries, the cutting of income tax and other such policies which liberated the individual from all-too-pervasive state control.

Key Points

As you read this chapter, ask yourself:

- Has the state reduced the rights of individuals during recent decades?
- If so, why has this happened?
- Were the Conservatives of the 1980s and1990s particularly blameworthy?
- How justified was the alleged clamp down in areas such as policing, combating terrorism, secrecy and broadcasting?

- How different is a leftwing and rightwing concept of liberty, in the light of the experience of these years?

A DEVELOPING CLIMATE OF RESTRICTION

In the last two decades, there has been growing anxiety that political freedoms in Britain are being eroded. It is convenient to see the Conservative victory in 1979 as the event which triggered the process and indeed several statutory initiatives and other measures by the executive branch restricted traditional liberties. Yet before the election of the Thatcher government, there were measures which were widely viewed by civil libertarians as repressive.

It was a Labour government which in 1968 imposed restrictions on British passport holders who wished to enter Britain, by passing the Commonwealth Immigrants Act. It was Labour which, in office from 1974–79, among other things:

- sought to prevent the publication of the *Crossman Diaries*, an exposé by a Cabinet minister of the way in which government works;
- introduced the Prevention of Terrorism Act in the light of the Birmingham pub bombings;
- used the immigration procedures established by the Conservatives in 1971 to deport two Americans, Philip Agee and Mark Hosenball, on grounds of national security (in the case of Hosenball he was given no explanation as to why his expulsion was conducive to the public good).

However, it is in the years since 1979 that there have been far more examples of the erosion of civil liberties which have significantly affected the relationship between the individual and the state. In particular, the growing incidence of restrictions has been in response to fears about national security. The threats of terrorist activity and the relentless increase in the amount of crime have led to demands for tougher action to clamp down on those responsible, and to limit the opportunities which encourage such actions. In so doing, however, the danger is that the rights of innocent people are curtailed, and that democratic values of freedom are undermined.

POLICE POWERS

There have long been anxieties about the conduct of the police in Britain, and from the establishment of the Metropolitan Force in 1829 onwards there have always been those who see a professional police as alien to British traditions. Gradually, the necessity for such a force was recognised, and McCrudden and Chambers offer an explanation of why this came about:

> *Central to acceptance of the force by the majority of the public was the belief that the police were subordinate to the rule of law, and that they lacked either legal powers or the coercive capacity to police other than by the consent of the populace. This is the...concept of the police as 'citizens in uniform', which played a focal part in the reports of both the 1929 and 1962 Royal Commissions on the Police.*

The concept may have been attractive as an ideal, but for many years it has been accepted that the police have powers which are significantly different from those of the ordinary citizen. They are now much greater than they were in the prewar era. Their manpower and resources have increased considerably, and so has their legal authority.

From 1979, members of the new Conservative government tended to view the police as the 'thin blue line' which was the last bastion preventing the country from descending into anarchy. Accordingly, their position needed to be strengthened. Much of the concern since then has been about the balance between those additional powers seen as necessary to bring about increased effectiveness, and the adequate machinery of safeguards to ensure the right of individual liberty.

The Conservatives relied on the police to maintain order on the streets in times of inner city rioting, to combat football hooliganism, and to monitor the activities of those engaged in various forms of public protest or who led a free-and-easy lifestyle of travellers. In the attempt to discipline trade unions, and especially during the Miners' Strike of 1984–85, the police were used extensively not only to deal with picketing and the possibility of mob violence, but also to control the movement of flying pickets around the country. Their activities were often much criticised by groups concerned with protecting established rights. In the policing of an anti-National Front demonstration in 1979, the teacher Blair Peach was killed by a Special Patrol Group officer; in the riots in Brixton and Toxteth in 1981, the police were alleged to have broken into people's homes and assaulted them; in the Miners' Strike there were hundreds of complaints ranging from illegal detention to the tapping of union members' phones, from the strip-searching of miners' wives to wilful damage of their homes.

There were other incidents too numerous to itemise, but they included cases of suspects being assaulted in custody, the misuse of firearms, the shooting of innocent people, as well as repeated evidence of corruption and the falsification of evidence in cases such as those of the Guildford Four and the Birmingham Six. The former were released in 1989, having served 14 years for involvement in IRA pub bombings. The latter case caused particular unease, after it was found that members of the West Midlands Serious Crime Squad had been guilty of the use of intimidation, the extraction of false confessions and the manufacturing of evidence in their attempts to ensure the original convictions. Such was the scale of its abuse of power in this and other cases that the Squad was disbanded by the Chief Constable in 1989.

THE BIRMINGHAM SIX ON THEIR RELEASE, 15 MARCH 1991. THEY WERE IMPRISONED FOR 25 YEARS BUT RELEASED 17 YEARS AFTER THEIR CONVICTION ON THE GROUNDS THAT THE FORENSIC EVIDENCE AND POLICE METHODS WERE 'UNSAFE'

There were many surveys which pointed to decreasing public confidence in the police, and concern about their activities. Some commentators went so far as to describe Britain as a 'police state'. If such language seemed over-dramatic, nonetheless the attack on police behaviour came not only from the more predictable sources such as Arthur Scargill, but also from eminent lawyers and judges, as well as from church persons such as the Bishop of Durham. Lord Gifford, QC, wrote during the Miners' Strike of 'police state measures which would be condemned as outrageous if they were being imposed on coal miners in Poland'. Writers regularly pointed to the use of force, the militarisation and politicisation of the police, and the arbitrary nature of law enforcement. Trade unionists, nuclear disarmers, young and black people, and hippie travellers seemed to be especially vulnerable to heavy-handed policing.

LEGISLATION ON POLICE POWERS

The Conservatives still took the view that it was necessary to enhance the position of the police, and the Police and Criminal Evidence Act (1984), known more usually as PACE, is widely recognised to have been a watershed, involving a considerable strengthening of police powers. Among other things, the Act allowed the police to detain suspects without charge for four days and deny them access to a solicitor for 36 hours. 'Stop and search' powers were extended, enabling the police to set up roadblocks; some 70 were erected in the Nottingham area alone, during the Miners' Strike.

The Public Order Act (1986) provided new definitions of – and sentences for – disorderly behaviour, unlawful assembly and rioting. It also gave the police new rights over the conduct of marches and processions, including the right to ban demonstrations if they were viewed as a threat to public order or a 'serious disruption to the local community'.

The Criminal Justice and Public Order Act (1994) involved many issues of concern to civil libertarians, and was described by a Liberty spokesperson as the 'most serious and broad-ranging assault on human rights' for many years. Introduced by the Home Secretary Michael Howard, it imposed new restrictions on the granting of bail, expanded police powers to ban public assemblies and crack down on 'raves' and travellers, established new offences of trespass, set up a national DNA database, and created new police rights to take intimate body samples. More well known than many other provisions was the restriction on the right to silence which had been widely seen as a cornerstone of criminal justice in Britain (see p 47).

PROTEST AGAINST THE CRIMINAL JUSTICE AND PUBLIC ORDER ACT (1994)

A further Conservative measure, part of the package produced by Michael Howard, was the Police Act (1997), which eventually passed in a modified form. The opposition of some senior members of the judiciary and many other public figures helped to push the Labour opposition to adopt a more critical stance, and gain concessions. They were alarmed at the power given to the police to authorise themselves to enter private premises, plant bugs, inspect files, and do many other things in pursuit of their criminal investigations, for such things seemed to be an assault on the citizen's freedom from arbitrary intrusion into his or her property – a liberty protected for more than 200 years.

THE RIGHT TO SILENCE

The Runciman Commission on Criminal Justice (1994) had recommended that the right should remain, as had previous ones in 1929 and 1981. But the Major government introduced new legislation to end the existing situation. The Home Secretary claimed that the accused currently had too much of an advantage over those prosecuting. In a sense the right to silence is bound to remain in spite of the legislation, for no-one can be forced to answer questions in a police station. But whereas previously the court could not infer guilt if the right was exercised, the silence can now be taken into consideration when the question of innocence or guilt is being debated. Anyone who stays silent is now taking a significant risk.

To opponents of the government, this was a serious blow to the traditional presumption that a person is innocent until proven guilty. They argued that there was little evidence that the conviction of terrorists or other serious criminals was being impeded by the right, and felt that the measure was unnecessarily draconian. They pointed out that, under heavy and intimidatory questioning, silence at the police station might be the natural course for people overwhelmed by the circumstances. In 1993, Michael Mansfield, QC, explained his fears in the *Guardian*:

Confessions are the worst and most unreliable form of evidence you can find and should be regarded as no evidence at all...Instead of increasing the risk of false confession by encouraging detainees to speak, we should be looking towards stringent and enforceable rights and protections, while encouraging criminal investigation quite independent of the words of the suspect. False confessions are regularly forthcoming in conditions of isolation, custody, tension, fear, emotional and mental confusion, personality disorder and educational inadequacy. [In the words of one person wrongly imprisoned]; 'I was frightened, so I just told them what I thought they wanted to know'.

The Guardian, 6.10.93

During the passage of the Criminal Justice and Public Order Bill, one MP, John Fraser, made the point that 'if we had a written constitution, the right to silence would be part of it. It is a right which has found its way into the constitutions of several countries where the British legal system has been copied'. The official Labour opposition had little to say on the Bill, and it was mainly in the Lords that there were voices expressing alarm. The then Lord Chief Justice, Lord Taylor, was publicly critical, and it was the *Observer* which noted in 1994 that:

> *If it were not for he and some fellow peers, measures which jeopardise judicial independence and go to the heart of the relationship between the individual and the State would be passing virtually without debate*
>
> *The Observer, 23.1.94*

In the opinion of representatives of several civil liberties groups, the clauses in the 1994 Act concerning the right to silence were probably in breach of the European Convention, Article 6, which entitles defendants to be presumed innocent until proven guilty and to have a fair and free trial. The presumption of innocence appears to be gravely affected, for a jury is being invited to draw an inference of guilt; juries may assume that an innocent person would give evidence if he or she has nothing to hide.

CONCERN ABOUT PRESENT-DAY POLICING

Opposing the 'law and order' lobby has been an active array of penal reform and civil liberties groups, and Liberty, the Howard League, Justice and a range of single-issue groups based upon alleged miscarriages of justice in specific cases, have urged the need for investigation of particular incidents. Most people will concede that the police need a range of powers to enable them to carry out effective investigations, but the fear is that the safeguards over how they are exercised have been insufficient. The balance between powers and individual freedom has moved significantly in the last few years and, in the 1980s especially, the police have been involved in a series of controversial manoeuvres to control industrial, political and mob violence, as well as their more traditional work of combating the more usual forms of day-to-day crime. It was the maintenance of public order during such disturbances which was the most overtly political role of the police. The additional powers granted to them in this area were highly contentious.

So too are the powers granted in the Police Act (1997). During discussion on the Bill, the extent of police 'bugging' and 'burgling' became apparent. The *Guardian* revealed that during 1995 the police took part in 1,300 covert bugging operations in England and Wales, many of which would have required the investigating officers to break into premises – homes and offices – surreptitiously. Strangely, although the police require a ministerial warrant to bug a telephone, this procedure is unnecessary when breaking into and bugging a private home. The powers of the police were substantially widened in the new Act. Previously, they could only use bugs when more normal methods had been tried and failed, and there was a likelihood of an arrest and conviction following their employment. Now, bugging and burglary can be authorised when they are likely to be 'of substantial value', and the police are satisfied that the desired outcome could not be achieved 'by other means'. Groups such as anti-road protestors or demonstrators against live calf exports could be vulnerable.

Once the necessary evidence is obtained, other potential infringements of rights follow. There are now some 130,000 police men and women in England and Wales, and between them they annually arrest more than 1 million people a year, compared with 1.4 million in 1979. By its very nature, each arrest involves a serious deprivation of personal liberty. The events which follow – detention in the police station, the release or non-release on bail, the time-lag between arrest and being brought to trial, the nature of the interrogation and the way in which they are conducted – have serious implications for civil liberties. In the words of Geoffrey Robertson:

> *The rules which govern police conduct at this point are our basic protections for personal freedom and are our most important safeguards against forced or fabricated confessions. We look to the law to ensure that no person is arrested without substantial cause, and that those suspects detained in police custody are treated fairly. Otherwise, there is a danger that justice will miscarry – either because the innocent are convicted on the strength of false confessions, or because the guilty are acquitted by juries who refuse to believe confessions extorted by police misbehaviour.*
>
> Freedom, the Individual and the Law

The difficulty is to maintain a balance between society's need to apprehend those who commit anti-social behaviour and can cause enormous injury to person and damage to property, and the rights of the accused: between creating the necessary conditions for order without being so restrictive as to limit the rights of people to live their daily lives without undue interference.

THE PREVENTION OF TERRORISM

The value of the Prevention of Terrorism Act (PTA), passed in the aftermath of the Birmingham pub bombings by a Labour government, has been hotly contested. It was originally rushed through the House of Commons, and passed after a mere 40 hours of debate. The Act continued with bipartisan support until 1983, when Labour began to challenge the arbitrary nature of its powers. Labour has criticised it for many years, although as a gesture to demonstrate its abhorrence of terrorist activity it abandoned its formal Parliamentary opposition in 1996 when the measure came up for its annual renewal.

Anxiety centres primarily on the power to detain suspects in police custody without trial for a period up to seven days. Some critics could accept the prolonged detention if an order to extend the time beyond 48 hours was made in a judicial review in the courts, rather than by the Home Secretary. Another area of concern is the use of 'exclusion orders' under which the same minister has the power to expel someone from Britain to Northern Ireland, or vice versa. Known popularly as 'internal exile orders', these controls bar selected British citizens living in Ulster from travelling to the mainland.

It is argued that the ratio of charges to arrests shows that many people are detained, even though there is little likelihood of their case standing up in court – as the figures from the Home Office illustrate:

Table 2: *Total numbers of people detained, excluded and charged under the Prevention of Terrorism Act and other emergency legislation*				
YEAR	NUMBER	EXCLUSION ORDERS MADE	CHARGED WITH PTA OFFENCE/OTHER OFFENCE	RELEASED
1984	159	1	14	135
1987	184	15	9	152
1990	169	14	6	130
1993	145	4	5	111
1996	84	24	17	43

SOURCE: HOME OFFICE STATISTICAL BULLETIN, FEBRUARY 1997

That far more people are arrested than are actually charged with an offence seems to indicate a misuse of PTA powers. The observation of a former Home Secretary, Leon Brittan to a TV journalist in 1985 explains that this is so;

> *I think that is a very misleading figure because that suggests that the purpose of detention is simply to bring a charge. If that were so, there might almost be no need for the legislation. What the figures do not tell you is how much information was obtained, not only about the people concerned but about others, and how many threats were averted as a result of obtaining information from those who were detained. The object of the exercise is not just to secure convictions, but to secure information.*
>
> *This Week, Radio Telefís Eireann, June 1985*

The period of detention – and the circumstances under which it is allowed – are much disputed, and featured in a judgement in Strasbourg. In 1988, in one of its most well-publicised verdicts, the European Court found Britain to be guilty of a breach of human rights over its use of the PTA. Four men who had been held under the Act for between four and seven days and then released without charge were adjudged to have been unfairly treated by the authorities, for – amongst other things – their experience fell foul of the requirement in Article 5 (3) that anyone arrested for terrorist offences should be taken 'promptly before a judicial authority'. They sought, but did not win, compensation from the British Government; it was felt that the finding of a violation was in itself 'just satisfaction'.

In the Brogan case, as it is usually known, the Court rejected ministers' views that special features should apply in the context of Northern Irish terrorism, and declared that on each count brought there had been a violation. Ministers disagreed, and the British Government did not change the law on detention as it would have been expected to do in the light of the ruling. Instead, it exercised its right to derogate from its obligations, using the claim that in the province there was a 'public emergency affecting the life of the nation'. The decision to derogate was not technically a breach of international law, but it has been widely condemned by libertarian groups such as Amnesty International and Liberty. As the original derogation on events covering Ireland made in 1957 had been withdrawn in 1984, and as there was no obvious increase in the dangers of the situation over the next few years, it is difficult to see the legitimacy of British policy.

SECRECY

Secrecy is another area in which it is felt that the changes of the 1980s were unduly restrictive. Secrecy is a well–observed feature of British Government and has been for most of the twentieth century. Governments have been determined to clamp down on the release of information and have been unwilling to supply information which many feel should be in the public domain – except when it is let out by unattributable leaks from ministers or in off-the-record briefings of journalists. The view taken by those in authority has been that expressed by Sir Humphrey in the political satire *Yes Minister*: 'Open government is a contradiction in terms. You can be open, or you can have government'. Whereas other countries from Australia to the USA, from Canada to Sweden, have freedom of information legislation, in Britain the legislation has been to prevent unwarranted disclosure.

THE OFFICIAL SECRETS ACT (1911)

The initial Official Secrets Act of this century was passed in 1911. It was deliberately intended to be draconian in its clamp down on any civil servant who felt it necessary to speak to the press, and Section Two became notorious as a catch-all clause forbidding any unauthorised disclosure of information even down to such trivial items as a Ministry of Defence luncheon menu. Much condemned, it applied to any person having in his or her possession information which was obtained whilst that person was holding a position under Her Majesty. Any leakage was a criminal offence. Yet it was little used in the generation after the First World War, and from 1945 to 1971 there were still only 23 prosecutions. Indeed, in the 1970s it appeared that prosecutions under the Act had fallen into disuse. However, interest revived in the 1980s and between 1978 and 1986 there were 29 prosecutions, and although some of these were unexceptionable (as the police officer who provided information to a burglar alarm company on local crimes) others seemed less concerned with national security and more concerned with saving the government from political embarrassment.

MERITS AND DISADVANTAGES OF OPEN GOVERNMENT

In Britain, there have been limited signs of greater openness in government, stemming from the more liberal Code of Practice adopted in 1994. But the Thirty Year Rule and other statutes prohibiting disclosure remain, and the categories which are exempt from the Code are wide in scope, covering items ranging immigration issues to law enforcement, from legal procedures to individual privacy and – more predictably – from defence to national security.

In favour of a more open system is the argument that it is beneficial to good government. Excessive secrecy may undermine faith in the authority and fairness of government, by fuelling suspicions that there is much waste, inefficiency or even corruption going on behind the scenes. The more policies and their implications are fully unveiled and debated in an informed manner, the more likelihood there is of a wise decision being made. Greater openness would also act as a restraint upon ministers and officials, for they would know that their decisions have to be capable of convincing justification. Beyond these considerations, there is the basic 'right to know' in a modern democracy; people are entitled to understand better the outlook and actions of those who rule over them. If particular groups such as disadvantaged or unpopular minorities know why a particular decision has been made, it might help to allay their fears and anxieties. Pressure groups representing them would be in a better position to present their members' causes effectively.

In Britain, ministers have been reluctant to open up the processes of government, whatever they may have once said in opposition. In the debates on the Scott Report in 1996 (Hansard), it was remarked that the 'legalistic approach' of freedom of information regimes is 'inflexible in...application and...expensive' for users. Or again, as Norton-Taylor comments in the discussions the Matrix Churchill case in 1989, it was said that to reveal documents or oral evidence which provided 'honest and candid advice' for ministers would be 'against the public interest', perhaps because of the danger that ill-informed criticism might colour the tone of public debate. Another view is that open government would slow the decision-making processes of government. In the words of a former official, Lord Bancroft: 'Government is difficult enough already, without having to halt continually while people peer up the governmental kilts'.

To those who dislike the cult of secrecy, the arguments in its favour are simply an excuse for making life easier for ministers who are denied the necessity of facing hostile public reaction to their ideas. To its defenders, it is essential that civil servants feel free to offer frank opinions to their ministers, and that their actions remain anonymous. Ministers take the blame for what goes wrong.

Tisdall and Ponting

Two well-known cases in the early 1980s were those concerned with Sarah Tisdall and Clive Ponting. In the former, the young woman involved was a clerk in the Foreign Office. She photocopied departmental documents concerning the delivery of cruise missiles to the Greenham Common defence base, and passed them to the *Guardian*. Her identity was eventually ascertained, and she was prosecuted under Section Two and sent to gaol.

In the other case, Clive Ponting, a senior official in the Ministry of Defence, who was much involved with day-to-day Naval matters of staff and policy, became a hero among many civil libertarians. His leak of information was more damaging to the government than Sarah Tisdall's had been, for he revealed documents to an MP which cast serious doubt upon government pronouncements on the sinking of the General Belgrano, an Argentinian vessel in the Falklands War. He was convinced that the House and indirectly the people were being deceived by ministers, and took the view that it was in the public interest that this was brought to light.

There was no question of any danger of national security; rather, it was a question of a breach of confidentiality. In the resulting trial, jury vetting, the taking of some evidence in camera and an arbitrary summing up by the judge who damned Ponting's case, were important features. But the central point was whether it was in the interests of the state for him to reveal such information. This was a rarely used defence, and one that was thought unlikely to save him from imprisonment. For he admitted that he had communicated confidential information to an unauthorised person. Yet in spite of the oppressive tone of Section Two the jury found him not guilty, a vindication of the 'public interest' defence which Ponting's counsel had deployed. The machinery of the state to tackle issues of public confidentiality seemed to be in disarray. Reform of the Official Secrets Act (OSA) seemed more than ever necessary.

THE OFFICIAL SECRETS ACT (1989)

The 1989 measure made it much easier for the state to deal with cases which proved to be difficult prosecutions under the old measure. Whereas for years Section Two had not been taken quite seriously, the new bill could not be so easily written off. In the narrower but more vital areas of information which it seeks to protect, the public interest defence used by Ponting has been removed. Even a disclosure of information involving fraud, neglect or unlawful activity cannot now be defended as being in the public interest. It is therefore much easier to convict persons once they are brought to trial.

Critics of the 1989 Act argue that if people can be prosecuted in the public interest, then they must be entitled to defend themselves by citing the public interest. They argue that there are times when to reveal information is the only way for attention to be drawn to a serious threat to public safety. For instance, it could be desirable to expose a defence scandal, even at the risk of some danger to national security.

The Spycatcher case

State security became something of an obsession in the 1980s. But of the many cases which reached the courts it was the *Spycatcher* saga which probably caused the government the greatest embarrassment. Peter Wright's book on the security services caused a furore, for his memoirs provided a frank account of his earlier work as a security officer. Some of the allegations were rather stale and unremarkable, but there were more serious suggestions as well. Claims were made that the former head of MI5 was a Soviet double-agent, that the organisation had been involved in the burglary and bugging of trade unions and political parties, that there had been attempts to assassinate the Egyptian President Nasser in the Suez Crisis, and that an attempt had been made to destabilise the Wilson government in the mid-1970s. At a time when the activities of the security services were already receiving adverse publicity, the account fuelled criticism of the lack of accountability of those who controlled operations.

At the time of publication, Wright was living in Tasmania so that he was well removed from the jurisdiction of British courts. Ministers went to extraordinary lengths to prevent the book from being published, fighting the case firstly in Australia and then in Britain. The Official Secrets Act (1911) could not be used against him in a battle overseas, and the Government had to rely on a civil law action of breach of confidence, a law previously used mainly on matters of private and personal rights such as marital revelations and trade secrets.

Some papers such as the *Observer*, the *Sunday Times* and the *Guardian* were restrained from commenting on aspects of the affair until in October 1988 the House of Lords declared that the Attorney General was no longer entitled to an injunction. The issue went to the European Court in Strasbourg which gave its verdict in November 1991. There it was decided that in attempting to prevent the three papers from disclosing the evidence of wrongdoing by MI5, the government was violating Article 10 of the Convention, the one guaranteeing freedom of expression and information. The Court upheld the principle of prior restraint, thus supporting the government's initial injunctions to stop publication of Mr Wright's allegations. However, it argued that once *Spycatcher* revelations had been published in the USA in July 1987 the contents were available elsewhere and should have been made available to the British public.

IRELAND AND THE MEDIA

During the 1970s and 80s the relationship between security and the media's coverage of events in Ireland was a frequent theme. There was an obvious security implication in discussion of events in the province, and coverage often caused problems for broadcasters; it was their instinct to probe controversial and dramatic occurrences, and find out what had really happened. Ministers, on the other hand, were sometimes keen to suppress open reporting, at times out of a desire to display their backing for the security forces and on other occasions to avoid giving publicity to the IRA or other terrorist groups. Labour had previously had disagreements with those who controlled the media, and in 1976 the Secretary of State for Northern Ireland had accused the BBC of disloyalty in the fight against terrorism. Tory ministers more frequently found themselves at odds with journalists, and the Corporation in particular was subjected to heavy direct and indirect pressure.

The programme *Real Lives* was one which proved to be a cause of contention. In it, two people (one from either side of the religious divide) were portrayed and interviewed in their different settings, to give a picture of life in the two communities, Catholic and Protestant. After an intervention by the Home Secretary, the programme was postponed and shown in a very slightly modified form later in 1985. *Death on the Rock*, a Thames Television production in 1988, also caused offence to the Government. The programme dealt with the shooting of three IRA activists in Gibraltar by the SAS, and suggested that the shootings were unlawful as the victims were not behaving illegally at the time, or posing a threat to the security forces.

In the same year, Douglas Hurd, the next Home Secretary, imposed a ban on the broadcasting of free speech by representatives of certain organisations, notably Sinn Fein, the Ulster Defence Association (UDA) and the paramilitaries. Programmes could in future include the 'reported speech' of such supporters, or an actor's voice could read a quotation, but they could not speak for themselves, because – according to ministers – this gave them 'the oxygen of publicity'. The ban was challenged in the courts and eventually taken (unsuccessfully) to the European Court, for in the view of journalists it prevented them from informing viewers and listeners fully and fairly. In November 1988, the *Guardian* noted that the government seemed incapable of understanding that:

> *the freedom of the press [and broadcasters] is not about the freedom of journalists but the liberty of the subject.*
>
> The Guardian, 17.11.88

In these and other cases, ministers were leaning heavily on the media to get programmes banned, delayed or modified. There were other examples too, which did not concern Northern Ireland but more general issues of national security. The *Secret Society* episode on the Zircon spy satellite and the radio series *My Country Right or Wrong* ran into similar difficulties. Indeed, from the Falklands War (1982) onwards, it seemed as though there was a systematic campaign by the Conservatives to bring the BBC in particular, to heel. Of course, there are legitimate concerns about the need to protect public order and national security, but there is a need for those who would seek to censor what is shown to show just how the specific item is a genuine threat. Critics of the Tory government in the era after 1979 felt that too often the cry of 'national security' was raised, and its use was seen as sufficient proof that broadcasting would constitute a danger. The ban on the use of IRA spokespersons, now lifted, was particularly controversial, and in the UN Human Rights Committee fell short of acceptable international standards as laid down in the Covenant. It was felt that whilst safeguarding national security was a legitimate and indeed necessary objective, nonetheless there was little evidence that the prohibition had anything to do with that the pursuit of that goal.

FREEDOM UNDER THE THATCHER AND MAJOR GOVERNMENTS: AN ASSESSMENT

THE DEFENCE

There are differing views about the alleged decline of political liberty in the 1980s and early 1990s. Tory ministers would claim that they did much in these years to add to the liberty of the subject. They would point to the freedoms which they introduced or extended, such as the right to buy a council house, to buy shares in the various privatisation sales, to choose a hospital, doctor, lawyer or school, to keep more of the money earned and in the case of trade unionists to decide on a leader and whether or not to strike. Margaret Thatcher was very quick to point to the government's achievements in this area, and dismissed any charge that her administration had become authoritarian. She claimed to be a firm believer in 'devolution to the individual citizen' (February 1989), claiming that people were fit to run their own lives. One of her Home Secretaries, Douglas Hurd, told the House of Commons in the same year that:

in many ways, we have added to the liberties of the British people. I feel like a Chancellor of the Exchequer who abolished every tax except two or three, and was then roundly abused for having introduced these two or three.

Ministers' concept of freedom did not extend to agreeing to the European Charter for Social Rights, later to become better known as the Social Chapter of the Maastricht treaty (see p 71). In its original form this would have conferred important rights in the social field affecting conditions of employment. Margaret Thatcher was dismissive of such a 'socialist charter', a policy continued by the Conservative government until its election defeat in 1997.

Her successor as Prime Minister, John Major, was the man who secured the opt-out from the Social Chapter at Maastricht, and he also disapproved of its 'creeping socialism' which he claimed threatened the competitiveness of British industry and exports by imposing new obligations on managers of small companies who would be unable to afford the extra burdens. His approach to matters of rights was to introduce the idea of the Citizens' Charter. He was more interested in providing people with rights as consumers, rather than extending their social entitlements. He felt that they could expect to have trains run on time, and hospital treatment offered within a reasonable period. Under his legislation, public services which failed to deliver good service were liable to pay compensation for the inconvenience and or hardship caused. A variety of charters followed, and these set out good practice in many fields. Other parties also developed an interest in the area of customer satisfaction, and tried to claim that they were more committed than the government because they understood that better services would only come about if more money was made available to the public sector.

The growing interest in consumerism serves to indicate just how wide-ranging is the subject of people's rights. But this approach, for which Conservative ministers were entitled to claim much of the credit, merely illustrates that there are very different concepts of rights between the political parties.

The rightwing defence of the Conservative record received enthusiastic backing from Kenneth Minogue, a Professor with rightist leanings at the London School of Economics (LSE) of rightist leanings (*Contemporary Record*). Noting disparagingly that critics often liked to portray the situation as though Britons were living as persecuted dissidents under the old Eastern European regimes, he observed that:

People vary in the freedoms they cherish. There are some who think compulsory membership of a trade union an interference with their liberty, while others think such membership the only option for a rational creature. Some value the freedom of terrorists to put their point of view on television, whilst others take the view that, by reinforcing the terrorist sense of its own power, such an opportunity leads in the long run to further death and maiming by an encouraged organisation.

THE ATTACK

Others are less convinced. Many organisations operating in the area of rights were concerned by the record of the Conservative government after 1979. They felt that there was an increase in governmental power at the expense of personal freedom. Liberty (formerly the National Council for Civil Liberties), launched an advertising campaign enumerating countless ways in which its members believed that the Thatcher governments had trampled on people's rights, under the title 'The more the government does, the less you're free to do'. It alleged that ministers had removed many of the freedoms which British people take for granted, adding that:

> *While it talks about rolling back the state, it has overseen a major increase in central government and police power. It has curtailed our right to peaceful assembly, to join a trade union, to elect our own local government, to receive information, to be free from discrimination. When these rights are taken from some, the freedom of all is threatened.*

Charter 88 was another body concerned with the subject of rights. Conservative ministers had little to offer on the matter of constitutional change designed to bring about a fundamental shift in the relationship between the individual and the state, and on matters ranging from the granting of devolution to Scotland and Wales (providing rights for the Scots and the Welsh to elect their own assembly) or the incorporation of the European Convention into British law, they were unwilling to budge. It was because of the lack of movement that Charter 88 was formed in 1988 to campaign for constitutional reform.

Among other things, Charter 88 urged for a change in the electoral system and a new Second Chamber. It also wanted to see a written constitution and a bill of rights. Many people of differing political persuasions signed the Charter, including artists, writers and an assortment of well-known public figures, as well as several politicians. They were concerned that the rights of the people no longer seemed to be inviolable, and believed that they needed to be enshrined in a written constitution. They urged incorporation of the European Convention as a way of giving citizens a clearer idea of their liberties, and also argued that such an action would have an educational force both on government behaviour and on the citizenry. The next generation would have a clearer idea of their freedoms, and minority and other disadvantaged groups would in the long term benefit particularly from this concern.

DIFFERING PERCEPTIONS

This section illustrates that there are very different views concerning what has happened to our liberties and rights in recent years. Whereas members of the

Conservative governments feel that they added to the sum of individual liberty, this view is challenged by those who believe that in key areas it was seriously eroded. The traditional freedoms of the person, expression, assembly and association, have been viewed as a poor second to the ones enunciated by Tories, and it is these with which we are primarily concerned. This is not to downplay the Conservative record in important areas, but to make the point that discussion of economic and social choices, which Conservatives admire, itself depends upon the existence of a core of basic civil liberties. As Ewing and Gearty (both left-inclined academics) point out in *Freedom under Thatcher*, those just referred to are important precisely because:

---

unlike the values promoted by the Conservatives, they have no political content. They are fundamental because they enable argument and debate about other matters to take place. The freedom to speak is not a freedom to say something in particular. The freedom to assemble is not the freedom to promote a particular point of view. [Such things] are the glorious facilitators of political debate. A nation that tampers with them risks its vitality and its originality. A government that does not believe in them threatens its country's well-being.

When British experience is compared with that in other countries, it becomes apparent that several other democracies have much less concentration of power at the centre and far more explicit protection for fundamental freedoms. To point to the many totalitarian countries which do not respect rights is no excuse for complacency. It is with other democracies that Britain should be compared, and in the following chapters we can see what has been done elsewhere to ensure respect for individual rights.

Some countries have opted for a bill of rights, but in the view of the above authors this would be cosmetic, a view to which we shall return. For them, there is a state of crisis. Whether it be in the extension of police powers, the restrictions on assembly and public protest, the growing emphasis on national security over individual rights, the assumption of extra powers to deal with Northern Ireland, or the less obvious cases involving no threat to security (the notorious Clause 28 which reduces the right of expression of gay men and women, the discriminatory legislation on matters of immigration and citizenship or the threat to the independence of the broadcasters), there is said to have been a spirit of intolerance in the air. If this is so, it poses a threat to liberties against which our existing safeguards may be thought to be inadequate.

CONCLUSION

It would be difficult to reach any consensus between the outlook of those on the Left and the Right on what happened to civil liberties in the years of

Conservative rule. Partly, the difficulty stems from different conceptions of freedom and disagreement about the rights which are important. It also reflects the sharply divergent opinions of the performance of the Thatcher and Major governments.

What may be said is that two trends emerge in the discussion. On the one hand, economic freedom and choice for the individual increased, and people were encouraged to assume greater responsibility for their own welfare. On the other hand, civil liberties – for reasons which may be regarded as justifiable or damnable – were decreased. In areas such as freedom of association, assembly and expression inroads were made, and the growing range of police powers indicated that ministers were more interested in clamping down on lawlessness than they were in preserving the rights of individuals and minorities.

Table 3: *Summary: Rights under threat, 1979 onwards*	
KEY DEVELOPMENTS	
1 Policing	Heavy reliance on police Increased police powers – 1984, 1986, 1994 and 1997 'Right to silence' inroads 'Police state'?
2 Terrorism	PTA: • Detention for up to 7 days • Internal exile orders
3 Secrecy	1911 OSA/prosecutions – e.g., Ponting case 1989 new OSA 'Obsession' with state security – *Spycatcher* No FoI legislation
4 Media	*Real Lives* Broadcasting ban *Zircon satellite/My Country Right or Wrong*

Overall
1   Increase of economic freedom/consumer protection
2   Restriction of civil liberties, dislike of social rights

STUDY GUIDES

Your notes need to focus on the relationship of the individual and the state in the years of Conservative rule. You need evidence of the changing situation, derived from several areas:

1 Police; Conservative support for and reliance upon police. Use for political purposes; key legislation of 1984, 1986, 1994 and 1997; right to silence.
2 Prevention of terrorism; reasons for introduction of PTA, its operation.
3 Secrecy; 1911 OSA ('catch-all' Section Two), 1989 change and its impact.
4 Media; Government pressure on broadcasters, especially re security issues.

Ensure that you are familiar with a rightwing and leftwing viewpoint.

Right: addition of new economic and consumer rights, lack of enthusiasm for social ones, less respectful of civil liberties (but dealing with key security issues)

Centre-Left: concern over threats to civil liberties, though Labour less hostile than Liberal Democrats to increased police powers in run-up to 1997 election.

The questions likely to be asked on recent concerns are of three main types. You may be asked a general question on the relationship between the individual and the state. The question may be more thought-provoking, along the lines of the example planned overleaf. Or it may be specific, on one area of the material covered in this chapter, perhaps a question on the growth in police powers or secrecy in government.

A visual plan can be a useful means of preparing an essay, and it has the advantage that points can be added as new thoughts arise. Such a plan helps to allow you to develop a logical argument. It is the analysis and evaluation rather than an excess of detail which will help you to score well, so you need to balance fact and comment, using the former to substantiate the latter. Overloading with fact tends to bury the argument, and the examiner is interested in your ability to tailor your information to the demands of the question set. Discipline yourself to be selective in the use of factual material, but provide good, up-to-date examples which are clearly explained.

See whether the type of plan given below helps you to arrange your material for the essay in such a way that every paragraph contributes a good point towards your argument. If this happens, your conclusion will then flow naturally from the case you have presented. By the way, such a diagrammatic approach can also be an aid to revision.

Essay Plan

INTRODUCTION

Concern over civil liberties growing over several years. Under last Labour Government, fears of growth of bureaucratic socialist state. When Tories in power, after 1979, more anxiety re respect for long-cherished liberties and rights. See views of Dworkin, Ewing and Gearty.

1   BILL OF RIGHTS

Growth of support for bill of rights over last 18 years. View no longer confined to isolated politicians and judges, but held by eminent members of judiciary, Lib. Dems. and more recently Labour Party, as well as organisations such as Charter 88 and Liberty.

2   THATCHER ERA

Feeling that Tory govt. insensitive to questions of individual freedom, examples concerning Police Act, PTA, GCHQ, Spycatcher, immigration policy etc.

3   FOUR KEY AREAS, 1979–90

Official Secrecy – 1989 Act; Media – attempts at control; threats to right of silence; Terrorism, PTA.

HAS THERE BEEN A CRISIS OF CIVIL LIBERTIES IN THE 1980s AND 1990s?

CONCLUSION

Situation has changed, with new govt. Labour committed to incorporating ECHR, FoI etc. Ban on unions at Cheltenham lifted. No reversal of economic rights, eg on sale of council houses. Talk of crisis, esp. now, alarmist.

4   MAJOR ERA

Further extensions of police powers, esp. CJA (1994) and 1997 Police Act. Howard and 'clampdown' on law-breakers. Growth of middle class protest re roads, animal rights etc.

8   A PROBLEM, BUT A CRISIS?

Crisis has implications of dramatic collapse in individual liberty, yet most essential freedoms intact. Need for vigilance, and to examine better protection for rights – eg need for bill of rights (ECHR?), FoI legislation etc.

7   DEFENCE OF TORY GOVERNMENTS

Overriding problem of state security, eg Ireland. Considerable increase in economic rights, eg of council house and share ownership.

6   EVIDENCE OF BRITISH RECORD IN STRASBOURG

Number of complaints to Commission; poor British record in European Court; surveys of UN Human Rights Committee; *The Democratic Audit* (Klug and co.).

5   TORY RULE OVERALL

Widespread feeling among academic critics (espec. on Centre-Left) that Tories, long in power, willing to ride roughshod over liberties Unwilling to act to secure social rights, eg of immigrants and racial minorities. More concerned with economic and property rights.

Group Work

Small groups might be asked to take one particular theme. They might research the issues involved in, say, changing police powers, and choose a speaker to present a talk which offers a survey of the main events\legislation and provides a reasoned defence or attack on the handling of the subject by ministers. A debate might be held at the end, on the motion that; 'This House believes that the Conservatives sharply diminished individual freedom in the years between 1979–1997.

Practice Questions

1 'Civil rights seem to be less securely established today than they were a generation ago'. Discuss
2 What problems have been caused by laws such as the Prevention of Terrorism Act and the Official Secrets Act in reconciling the values cherished in a liberal democracy with the protection of national security?
3 How fair is it to argue that if members of the public are to be protected by the police, then it is also necessary that they should be protected from the police?
4 'Police powers have increased, are increasing and ought to be diminished'. Discuss.

Glossary

Authoritarian rule   High-handed behaviour by those in authority who favour a more ordered society and are insensitive to matters of personal liberty

Arbitrary power   Power exercised in a dictatorial and maybe unpredictable manner

Confidentiality   Keeping public affairs out of the public domain; protecting sources

Derogate   To limit the application of a law; eg to find reasons to opt-out of its provisions

Inviolable   Cannot be dishonoured or broken

Police state   A state where the law is arbitrarily enforced by the police who are themselves largely above the law, behave in an authoritarian manner and have extensive powers of stop, search, detention and interrogation which are largely used in tacit or open support of the government of the day

Further Reading and Resources

Dworkin, R. (1990), *A Bill of Rights for Britain*, Chatto & Windus

Ewing, K. and Gearty , C. (1990), *Freedom under Thatcher*, Clarendon Press

Holme, R. and Minogue, K. 'Controversy: Are rights under threat in Britain?', *Contemporary Record*, Autumn 1989, pp 26–8

Robertson, G. (1995), *Freedom, the Individual and the Law*, Penguin

4

INTERNATIONAL OBLIGATIONS

Introduction

THE ABHORRENCE FELT by many people over the barbarism of the Second World War led to a determination that measures should be taken to prevent such brutality from ever recurring. In the postwar era, procedures for the protection of rights have been elaborated under the auspices of several international agencies, and these include the United Nations Organisation, the International Labour Organisation, the Conference on Security and Cooperation in Europe, the European Union and the Council of Europe. Britain is a member of all of these bodies, and therefore has commitments under the agreements into which past governments have entered.

Key Points
As you read this chapter, ask yourself:

- How committed is Britain to each international body? Have we ratified and/or incorporated its rights documents?
- Is its word binding in British law?
- Would we be better-off if we included it in British law?
- Which of the forms of international commitment provide the best protection of rights?
- Is the area of rights one in which 'the European solution' is desirable?

THE UNITED NATIONS AND ITS MACHINERY

The UN was destined to play a leading role in the protection of rights. In the UN Charter, there is a commitment to the promotion of human rights and emphasis is placed on the need for nations to respect them. In 1946, after establishing a

Commission on Human Rights, a decision was taken by the Economic and Social Council to devise an international bill of rights. On the day before it was adopted, a Convention on the Prevention and Punishment of the Crime of Genocide had already been backed by the General Assembly. However, it is the Universal Declaration of Human Rights, and the two International Covenants agreed in 1966 (one on civil and political rights, the other on cultural, economic and social ones), which are the most important and well-known.

The Declaration is non-binding, but it has considerable moral standing. There were those who, at the outset, wished to turn it into a covenant, with the intention that those states which ratified it would be legally committed. But this effort was lost in the atmosphere of the Cold War which was then developing. Countries were unenthusiastic about agreeing to any machinery which might tread upon their national sovereignty and encourage interference in their internal affairs. Because of this, little was done about the establishment of an international bill of rights which would be legally binding. Not until 1966 was an agreement concluded, and it was another ten years before it became operative.

Of the two covenants of that year, **the International Covenant on Civil and Political Rights** (the ICCPR) and the **International Covenant on Economic, Social and Cultural Rights** (the ICESCR), the western states were more sympathetic to the former and the old Soviet bloc to the latter. It was open to countries to ratify either or neither, but many opted to support both of them. Given the atmosphere of the times, it was unlikely that there would be strong enforcement machinery, although in theory the covenants are binding.

THE HUMAN RIGHTS COMMITEE

Those countries which have ratified either document are committed to little more than to report periodically on their record of compliance with its provisions. They may also (in the case of the ICCPR) have opted to allow the Covenant's Human Rights Committee to listen to complaints from other states and their own nationals about their failure to adhere to the terms of the agreement. In the case of complaints by other states, a friendly settlement may be encouraged, and in the case of individuals the Committee may adjudicate upon the petition. Britain has not signed the optional protocol which allows this right of individual petition, arguing that individual rights are better protected by the European Convention. Thus Britain merely makes occasional reports to the Committee, and undergoes questioning by its members about its performance.

The Human Rights Committee has existed since 1977, and so far Britain has submitted four reports to it (1977, 1984, 1989 and 1994). The first report showed that there was concern about Britain's record on matters relating to discrimination and the lack of equality of opportunity. In particular, anxiety was expressed about the situation in Northern Ireland, and the high unemployment rates experienced by Catholics compared to those of Protestants. It was also felt that immigration policy was radically discriminatory, and that conditions of prisoners – especially of those on remand – left much to be desired. Prisoners' rights, police powers, citizenship hights concerning entry into Britain, and rights of association concerned with the union closed shop featured in the 1984 report, and five years later the much lengthier review dwelt heavily on matters associated with terrorism, immigration, and racial and sexual discrimination – anxieties which were admitted by the British Government in its own report.

In assessing any report from a country which has ratified the Covenant, the Committee is entitled to take evidence from pressure groups with an interest in the field, and bodies such as Amnesty International, Charter 88, the Howard League for Penal reform, Justice and Liberty have all been active in publicising alleged lapses in British practice. The work of the Committee has been useful in drawing attention to both problems and progress in protecting rights and liberties, and the resulting reports and the reviews contain a wealth of material which illustrates the situation in countries which have committed themselves to such outside monitoring.

RECENT CONVENTIONS AND COVENANTS

More recently the UN drew up a Convention or Covenant against Torture, the idea of which had been agreed at the General Assembly in 1984. Other agreements concern such issues as the elimination of racial discrimination and of discrimination against women, the abolition of slavery, the   prevention of genocide and the status of refugees. After a decade of discussion, the General Assembly of the UN approved a Convention which was designed to protect the rights of children in the way that the 1948 Declaration looked after the position of adults. It came into force in September 1990, and has now been ratified by the overwhelming majority of countries.

Members of the UN pledge themselves to take collective and individual action to promote and encourage respect for human rights and basic freedoms. The Covenants they sign are legal commitments which they have entered into. Once ratified by 20 countries, they become part of international law. Any country which signs up for the Conventions must comply with their contents.

THE INTERNATIONAL LABOUR ORGANISATION

The International Labour Organisation (ILO) was originally established in 1919 as an international body with a wide remit in matters of employment welfare and workers' rights. In the post-1945 era, it has developed as an important piece of human rights machinery, though in a strictly limited area of activity. It reports to the Economic and Social Council, one of the political organs of the UN. Today, there are more than 170 members of the ILO, and Britain has been a member since its inception.

The General Conference attempts to influence standards of employment via the adoption of conventions and recommendations, and it also provides a valuable forum for the consideration of labour issues. The conference elects a Governing Body which has a two standing committees on human rights, the Freedom of Association Committee and the Committee of Experts on the Application of Conventions and Recommendations. The Governing Body may also decide to set up a special committee to investigate complaints concerning discriminatory practices in employment.

Table 4: *Key Conventions of the International Labour Organisation on Human Rights*	
1 **Convention 87**	Freedom of Association and Protection of the Right to Organise. In force since 1950, ratified by Britain.
2 **Convention 98**	Application of the Principle of the Right to Organise and Bargain Collectively. In force since 1951, ratified by Britain.
3 **Convention 100**	Equal Remuneration for Men and Women. In force since 1950, ratified by Britain.
4 **Convention 111**	Discrimination in Respect of Employment and Occupation. In force since 1960, not ratified by Britain.

BRITAIN AND UNITED NATIONS RIGHTS

British Governments have supported the UN effort to establish internationally recognised standards of behaviour in the area of rights. Britain has ratified a range of UN and ILO covenants and conventions. These include the two Covenants of 1966; the one against torture; the ones against racial and gender discrimination and the one on the rights of the child (in the latter case, there was a reservation on employment practices). It also signed up to the non-binding Universal Declaration of 1948. It has not incorporated any of the Covenants into British law.

In 1991, its representatives were elected for a three year period to serve on the Commission on Human Rights which investigates abuses in this area.

THE ORGANISATION FOR SECURITY AND COOPERATION IN EUROPE

In 1973, at a time when the Cold War was still in existence, the leaders of 34 of the western democracies and the communist peoples of eastern and central Europe met in Helsinki with a view to improving dialogue between the two sides. Two years later, an Helsinki Accord was signed, which among other things included a commitment to the pursuit of human rights and self-determination. Subsequently, more meetings were agreed, but it was the ending of the Cold War which brought about a new impetus for cooperation. The Charter of Paris signed in November 1990 restated the first principles of the Organisation for Security and Cooperation in Europe (OSCE), and stressed the importance of human rights, multi-party democracy and the rule of law.

The primary role of the OSCE is to promote international security; the importance of human rights issues is that breaches of standards set out in the Helsinki Accord can damage international relations. It has no binding machinery, and relies on pressure and reciprocity to bring about improvements. But in view of the states' desire to move forwards on the basis of consensus, there is a strong mutual interest in so conducting internal arrangements for human rights that nothing is done to jeopardise goodwill. In 1991, the Concluding Document of the Moscow Meeting stated that when nine other member countries agree, then any participating state is allowed to send its observers into another state where it has reason to believe that flagrant violations of rights are taking place.

THE EUROPEAN UNION

Although the European Convention (see pp 72–84) is by far the most impressive piece of European law to ensure that rights are respected, the treaties involved in the development of the European Union confer important rights. Certain categories of people benefit from aspects of Union policy, such as French agricultural workers whose standard of living has been protected by the Common Agricultural Policy (CAP). Again, the Treaty of Rome – many of the objectives of which are being fulfilled via the Single European Act (1986) – ensures freedom of movement and the transferability of professional qualifications throughout the EU.

Sometimes, problems have occurred on such topics, either because national laws are different, or because of the absence of specific legislation in some areas. Typical ones have included the non-recognition of qualifications, the unequal treatment of men and women, or disagreements over pensions and social security where the claimant has worked in more than one state. In these and other cases, petitions may be made to the European machinery. Anyone with a complaint which they wish to bring to the attention of the Community can do so by approaching either the European Commission, the European Parliament or the European Court of Justice.

Most cases get referred to Luxembourg by national courts. For instance, in early 1997 the British High Court decided to submit the case of a former serviceman sacked from the Royal Navy for being gay to the Court of Justice, on the grounds that this could well be a breach of European rules on equal treatment for men and women at work. Protection under the relevant directive has already been granted to trans-sexuals, and it is difficult to see how it can be withheld from those of homosexual orientation.

THE EUROPEAN PARLIAMENT AND RIGHTS

Most petitions are made to the European Parliament, the composition of which for many years was itself the denial of a basic right. It was not until 1979 that the first elections to it were held, so that for more than two decades the key principle of choice through universal suffrage was not implemented in the Community. Since then, the European Parliament's authority is founded upon the will of the people, even if in some countries many people do not exercise their right to vote.

The Parliament has established a Commission on Petitions, comprising 28 Members of the European Parliament (MEPs) who are interested in the question of citizens' rights. They reflect the balance of political leanings and national groups represented in the chamber. If the Committee finds the grievance admissible, it investigates to see if it is well-founded, and this may involve requesting relevant documents from the Commission. If the complaint is upheld, the President of the Parliament can then intervene with the body which denied justice (ie the Commission, Council or national authority), and ask that the matter be put right, or he can ask the Parliament to draw up a Resolution which requests that the appropriate authority takes the required action.

The Parliament has been a strong defender of women's rights, and has a permanent committee to examine matters in which these are not being fully acknowledged. Many issues have arisen out of a requirement of the Treaty of Rome that 'men and women should receive equal pay for equal work' (Article 119). The original provision was inserted in the Treaty because there was a feeling that without it some countries which had already made provision for equal wage rates would be at a competitive disadvantage to those where there was no such legislation. This is a good example of a move made primarily for economic reasons which has had the effect of moving the Union towards closer harmonisation and integration. In so doing, it has conferred important rights.

Table 5: *Petitions to the European Parliament: some Relevant Statistics*			
1 The increasing number of petitions in the past decade			
1987	**1990**	**1993**	**1996**
484	789	1051	1067
2 Nationality of the petitioners: the top five countries			
Germany	235		
Britain	148		
Italy	141		
France	118		
Spain	91		
3 Topics Covered			
Many now concern issues such as animal welfare and the environment, but womens' rights, civil liberties and consumer/benefits entitlements also continue to feature.			

SOURCE: THE OFFICE OF THE EUROPEAN PARLIAMENT

RECENT DEVELOPMENTS IN THE UNION CONCERNED WITH THE PROMOTION OF RIGHTS

For at least two decades, there has been occasional discussion of the ways in which the Community should advance in the area of human rights. Thought has been given to whether, as a whole, it should accede to the European Convention, but as yet this has not been done. The European Parliament did adopt a Declaration of Fundamental Rights and Freedoms in 1989, with the hope that this move would be followed by the other EC institutions and eventually by the whole Community.

The Maastricht Treaty on European Union

The signing and implementation of the Maastricht Treaty on European Union (TEU) in December 1991 has been significant in the area of rights. The document confirmed that those fundamental rights guaranteed by the European Convention must be respected by all signatories to the Treaty of Rome. Since the TEU came into force, a number of new rights have arisen. It was accepted at Maastricht that it was an important objective of the new Union 'to strengthen the protection of the rights and interests of the nationals of its Member States through the introduction of a citizenship of the Union'. Accordingly, people living in member countries have now become citizens of the EU. As a result, they have acquired additional voting rights. European citizens living in Britain are entitled to vote or be a candidate in Euro-elections in the same way that British nationals are allowed to do elsewhere in the Union. Also, since 1994, all European citizens are entitled to take part in municipal elections, though formal arrangements for this change have yet to be made.

The Social Chapter

A further development of considerable importance was the consideration given to what was originally known as the Social Charter and at Maastricht became the Social Chapter. Eleven states were prepared to sign this Protocol and Agreement on Social Policy which is not part of the main treaty, but Britain would not. The Conservative government saw the Social Chapter as an insidious form of socialism which would impose shackles on British industry and thereby limit competitiveness. The Labour Party and trade unionists had been converted to a more pro-European stance in the late 1980s precisely because they liked the way in which the then Community was beginning to embrace social policy as an area of concern. Once in office, Tony Blair quickly signed up to the Protocol which will eventually involve the creation of new social rights for British people.

The Social Chapter remains largely a set of aspirations, and as yet few initiatives have been taken under its auspices. However, two controversial measures have been adopted, to which Britain is now committed. These cover the right of workers to be represented in works councils, and the entitlement of women to maternity leave and men to have nine weeks off in the first year of their child's life. Worker protection for part-time and young workers, and better opportunities for women are likely to be the next matters provided via the Chapter. Other forms of worker protection can be tackled under the health and safety provisions which were agreed as part of the arrangements for the completion of the single market in 1992.

The Amsterdam Treaty

Finally, in the draft Amsterdam Treaty (June 1997), it was agreed that the Union would respect not only those rights guaranteed by the European Convention, but also those set out in the European Social Charter (see p 84). In addition, it was decided that the institutions of the EU would take action to promote the needs of persons with a disability, and that the Council of Ministers would be empowered to take appropriate action to combat discrimination based on sex, racial or ethnic origin, religion or belief, disability, age or sexual orientation.

THE COUNCIL OF EUROPE AND THE PROTECTION OF HUMAN RIGHTS

The Council of Europe was established in 1949, and was the first European political institution of the postwar era. Its aim was:

> *to achieve a greater unity between its members for the purpose of safeguarding and realising the ideals and principles which are their common heritage and facilitating their social and economic progress'*

The Council had another key goal, to work for the 'maintenance and further realisation of human rights and fundamental freedoms', and the creation of the European Convention on Human Rights and Fundamental Freedoms has been its most significant act. It believes that human freedoms are best upheld by countries which are effective democracies with a 'common heritage of political traditions, ideals, freedoms and the rule of law'.

THE EUROPEAN CONVENTION ON HUMAN RIGHTS

Drawing upon the Universal Declaration of the United Nations, the Council drew up its own treaty or convention, and members who ratified it were forced to acknowledge that individuals have rights under international law. The document is an international legal instrument drawn up in the belief that the freedoms to which individuals are entitled are best protected by a system of democratic government. Those who aspire to be members of the Council and signatories of the treaty need to be wedded to a common belief in freedom. The influence of this European initiative has been felt outside the continent, and has been the inspiration of other statements of basic liberties.

Fifteen nations signed the European Convention on Human Rights (ECHR) in November 1950, and the document came into force in 1953. Those who did so, or have done subsequently, accept that everyone within their jurisdiction enjoys the rights protected under the Convention. Today, there are 40 members of the Council of Europe, and all have signed up to the European Convention. In the 45 years of its operation, rights and obligations have been added to the original document, and states can choose which they wish to accept. Most have incorporated the Convention into their own legal system. Where this has not happened, as in Britain, a country's law should not conflict with it.

Table 6: *Member States of the Council of Europe at 28 February 1997*			
Albania	Estonia	Liechtenstein	Russia
Andorra	Finland	Lithuania	San Marino
Austria	France	Luxembourg	Slovakia
Belgium	Germany	Malta	Slovenia
Britain	Greece	Moldova	Spain
Bulgaria	Hungary	Netherlands	Sweden
Croatia	Iceland	Norway	Switzerland
Cyprus	Ireland	Poland	Macedonia*
Czech Republic	Italy	Portugal	Turkey
Denmark	Latvia	Romania	Ukraine
* former Yugoslav Republic			

The Contents of the Convention

Altogether, there were 66 articles in the original Convention, and since 1953 eleven Protocols have added new rights and obligations. The language employed is vague, deliberately so. More all-embracing phrases such as the 'right to liberty and security of person' (Article 5) and 'the right to freedom of peaceful assembly and to freedom of association with others' (Article 11) allow for interpretation, and enable complainants to include more of their grievances within its provisions. If the terminology was more precise, it would automatically exclude many issues from consideration. On the other hand, broad phrases require interpretation as to their application in individual cases, and such judgements are made by non-elected judges rather than by elected politicians.

The Convention draws upon the Universal Declaration of Human Rights, although the rights protected are less extensive. They include the classic civil and political rights, but unlike the ICCPR does not cover the protection of minority groups. Protection from discrimination is much weaker than it is under the International Covenant. A summary of its contents is listed and they include such terms as freedom of peaceful assembly and association, the right to form and to join a trade union, the right to peaceful enjoyment of possessions, freedom of thought, conscience and religion, the right of respect for privacy and the right to marry.

THE ARTICLES AND PROTOCOLS OF THE EUROPEAN CONVENTION:
A SUMMARY

Article 2	Right to life
Article 3	Prohibition of torture
Article 4	Prohibition of slavery and forced labour
Article 5	Right to liberty and security
Article 6	Right to a fair trial
Article 7	No punishment without law
Article 8	Right to respect for private and family life
Article 9	Freedom of thought, conscience and religion
Article 10	Freedom of expression
Article 11	Freedom of assembly and association
Article 12	Right to marry
Article 13	Right to an effective remedy
Article 14	Prohibition of discrimination
Article 25	Applications by persons, non-governmental organisations or groups of individuals
Article 28	Report of the Commission in case of friendly settlement
Article 31	Report of the Commission "if a solution is not reached"

Protocol No. 1

Article 1	Protection of property
Article 2	Right to education
Article 3	Right to free elections

Protocol No. 4

Article 1	Prohibition of imprisonment for debt
Article 2	Freedom of movement
Article 3	Prohibition of expulsion of nationals
Article 4	Prohibition of collective expulsion of aliens

Protocol No. 6

Article 1	Abolition of the death penalty

Protocol No. 7

Article 1	Procedural safeguards relating to expulsion of aliens
Article 2	Right of appeal in criminal matters
Article 3	Compensation for wrongful conviction
Article 4	Right not to be tried or punished twice
Article 5	Equality between spouses

SOURCE: TBS

For each article, the substantial right is expressed in the first paragraph. What follows in the second is a series of qualifications which list the exceptions to the application of the right. Thus, in Article 10, there is a clearly stated right to 'freedom of expression' which is then modified:

> *This right shall include freedom to hold opinion and receive and impart information and ideas, without interference by public authority and regardless of frontiers. This article shall not prevent States from requiring the licensing of broadcasting, television or cinema enterprises.*

In the second paragraph, there follows the important limitations listed as:

> *necessary in a democratic society, in the interests of national security, territorial integrity or public safety, for the prevention of disorder or crime, for the protection of health or morals, for the protection of the reputation or rights of others, for preventing the disclosure of information received in confidence, or for maintaining the authority and impartiality of the judiciary.*

The series of exceptions thus provide plenty of latitude to the Commission and the Court in interpreting the Convention, and in the early stages those who operated the machinery continued to rely on the state to decide the extent of the rights and its limits. After what McCrudden and Chambers call a 'confidence-building period', a more 'robust' approach has developed subsequently, 'as it has over prisoners' rights and sexual orientation'.

The Convention is generally considered to have been well drafted, though inevitably after more than 40 years in operation its broad provisions have sometimes been contentious. Few people would deny that the right to life, liberty and security of person is a basic one. The problem arises with particular cases, which call for an interpretation of what the phrase means in practice. As we have said, the interpretation is done by appointed judges rather than by elected politicians, and some people feel that this leaves too much scope to the judiciary to interpret articles in a restrictive manner.

There are features of the Convention which many people would now regard as undesirable. Some are politically contentious, and others might be considered politically obnoxious:

1 Article 5 qualifies 'the right to liberty and security of person' by allowing 'the lawful detention of persons for the prevention of the spreading of infectious diseases, of persons of unsound mind, alcoholics or drug addicts or vagrants'. This may seem to place arbitrary power in the hands of the authorities to detain people who have not committed a specific offence, but who have chosen to adopt an unconventional lifestyle. It seems to permit the detention of vagrants even if they have committed no specific offence, and in today's climate of opinion it may seem unfair to allow people to be taken into custody merely because of their chosen lifestyle. For instance, the clause could also permit the detention of people with diseases such as AIDS. Other articles might be questionable to political parties of the Left or Right.

2 Article 17 is similarly controversial: 'Nothing in this Convention may be interpreted as implying for any State, group or person any right to engage in any activity or perform any act aimed at the destruction of any of the rights and freedoms set forth herein, or at their limitation to a greater extent than is provided for in the Convention'. It has been argued by Wallington and McBride (and others) that this statement could be used to censor any expression of unpopular views.

3 Article 1 of the First Protocol states that: 'No-one shall be deprived of his possessions except in the public interest'. Although the article qualifies this with the proviso that a state's right to secure payment of taxes is not impaired, some have claimed that the clause could be quoted by someone willing to question the legality of a redistributive wealth tax, as distinct from a tax designed to raise revenue. The case has not been put to the test.

4 Article 2 of the same Protocol asserts that: 'No-one shall be denied the right to education...The state shall respect the right of parents to ensure such education and teaching in conformity with their own religious and philosophical convictions'. This could be interpreted as invalidating the abolition of private education, for abolition would require that the 'religious and philosophical convictions' of the parents were catered for within the public sector. Such a consideration has probably influenced the British Labour

Party in modifying its earlier stance on the ending of fee-paying schools. Some Conservatives might be uneasy about the clauses relating to freedom of 'assembly and association'.

As with any such listing of rights, there are bound to be unsatisfactory or doubtful features. The contents are not perfect, and if they were being redrafted today doubtless some rewording might be undertaken. However, given the difficulty in reaching agreement on any listing of rights, the document – for all its imperfections – provides a charter around which many supporters of civil liberties and human rights can rally. As Lord Hooson put it in a pamphlet back in 1977, 'if there were major flaws in its drafting, they could have come to light by now'. The Convention has the useful merit of already being in existence, having been broadly supported by both parties. Britain and other members of the Council of Europe are bound by its provisions.

Besides what are known as "the paragraph 2 exceptions", two general exemptions are placed on the rights of individuals. Article 15 allows a state to derogate from its obligations in circumstances of national emergency. This limitation applies only to certain articles such as that on terrorism – not to the right to be free from torture. Also, according to Article 17 (as quoted above) the rights guaranteed may not be used in such a way as to endanger the liberal values which the Convention wishes to uphold.

THE ENFORCEMENT MACHINERY

The European Commission on Human Rights

The Commission is the first port of call for those who wish to complain under the terms of the European Convention. This comprises one person from each state, the appointees being persons of a 'high moral character who have the necessary qualifications to serve in high judicial office'. They tend to be experts in national or international law. It does not sit continuously, but holds as many sessions per year as its workload dictates. In 1996, it held eight, each of two weeks. It is served by a permanent Secretariat of nearly 50 legal experts who can perform much of the initial work of sifting submissions, as well as providing specialised advice.

The Commission receives complaints from states or individuals and examines them for any breach of the Convention. Most complaints are from individuals under the right of individual petition (Article 25):

The Commission may receive petitions addressed to the Secretary General of the Council of Europe from any person, non-governmental organisation or group of individuals claiming to be the victim of a violation by one of the High Contracting Parties of the rights set forth in this Convention, provided that the High Contracting Party against which the complaint has been lodged has declared that it recognises the competence of the Commission to receive such petitions.

This feature of the machinery was a new one in international law, and not all states immediately ratified it; all present members have now done so. Before complainants can use this method of remedying their problem, they must have fully exhausted the machinery in their own country. They then have six months in which to apply.

From the setting up of the Commission in July 1954 to 31 December 1996, it received 34,297 individual applications. It now receives some 12,000 complaints every year, and more than one third of them are considered worthy of investigation to see if they are 'admissible' under the Convention. Before 'admissibility' can be decided, the Commission seeks information from all the relevant parties, and it is possible that an agreement may be reached at this stage without any further examination. If not, the Commission gives its verdict. Since its creation, roughly 10% of cases have been found admissible and worth proceeding with.

The Commission researches an admissible application, taking evidence from both sides to the dispute, hearing expert advice and doing any other necessary investigatory work. In some cases, a 'friendly settlement' can be negotiated; if not, a detailed report is produced which offers a preliminary judgement on whether or not the Convention has been violated.

Straightforward cases are sent to the **Committee of Ministers** and to the government/s involved. The Committee comprises one minister for each member state. Its role is a limited one, and much of its caseload concerns cases in which the relevant state concedes that a violation has occurred, and has made any necessary amendments to national law. More than 500 cases were brought to its attention in both 1995 and 1996. Some are referred to the European Court, but otherwise the Committee decides on any breach of the Convention. Its findings tend to echo those of the Commission. It can recommend that 'just satisfaction' or compensation is paid to the injured party, and its verdict is binding.

The European Court of Human Rights

In total, 784 cases were referred to the European Court up until the end of 1996. At present, individuals cannot directly approach the Court, though Protocol 9 will permit this in certain circumstances when it is enforced.

The Court comprises as many judges as there are member states, and no two judges may be nationals of the same country. A country can nominate a representative of a non-European state, as did Liechtenstein in 1990 when it selected a Canadian as its choice. Those appointed are expected to possess the same qualifications as those eligible for membership of the Commission.

A CASE HISTORY: SADO-MASOCHISM IN BRITAIN

The Bare Facts

Three middle-aged, homosexual men belonged to a group which indulged in sado-masochistic practices such as ritualistic beatings and branding. They fully consented to the infliction of pain upon them, and were happy to be filmed so that their activities could be shown in private viewings.

Legal Action in Britain

The police obtained copies of the videos, and the three men were charged with a range of offences under the Offences Against the Person Act (1861). The judge would not accept that their consent was a defence to the charges, and on pleading guilty, they were sentenced to periods of imprisonment of between one and three years. The Court of Appeal upheld their convictions (but lowered the sentences), and in 1993 the House of Lords similarly dismissed their appeal.

The European Solution:
The Commission

An application was lodged with the Commission on Human Rights in December 1992 under Article 8, and a part of their claim was declared admissible early in 1995 this deals with 'the right to respect for... private and family life'). An attempt to achieve a 'friendly settlement' failed, and the Commission therefore produced a report which established the facts and set out an opinion, namely that there had been no violation.

The Court

In the Court, it was commonly agreed that the applicants had suffered 'interference by a public authority' with their right to respect for private life, that this was carried out 'in accordance with the law' and that this was done for the 'protection of health or morals'. The issue was whether such interference was 'necessary in a democratic society'. It decided that the State was entitled to regulate the infliction of physical harm, and that it was up to the State's authorities to decide what was a tolerable level of harm. It did not accept that the behaviour was purely a matter of private morality, and noted that a significant degree of injury and wounding had occurred, and that there was potential for much greater harm. Accordingly the behaviour of the authorities was appropriate, and it was decided unanimously that there had been no violation of the Convention.

Before the Court considers a case, the country involved must have accepted its compulsory jurisdiction, as every signatory of the Convention has now done. Written and oral evidence is presented in Court, where legal aid can be available to a needy individual. The judges decide on whether a violation has occurred by a majority vote, and can award the victim 'just compensation'. Their verdict is a binding one, and implementation of the judgement is carried out by the Committee of Ministers.

CHANGES IN THE PROCEDURE

Because of the ever-growing number of cases which reach the Commission and the complex issues many of them raise, serious delays can occur. Often, it takes five or six years for the Court to give its verdict, so that the right to justice in a reasonable time is not fulfilled. On one occasion, it actually took 16 years.

The system has been collapsing under the weight of its own success, as its work has become so much better known. People over the continent have recognised its success in producing valuable verdicts on behalf of citizens. In 1995 and 1996 alone, 22,343 provisional files were opened by the Commission and examined for registration as to their eligibility. The Court itself now gives many rulings a year compared to one per annum in the first decade, as the figure indicate. Whilst in its first 18 years the Court delivered only 26 judgements, 472 were delivered over the next 18. The President of the Court was moved to comment in 1990 on a situation in which the machinery 'will no longer be able to cooperate in the way it does at present'. Protocol 9, allowing direct access to the Court in cases where the Commission has declared a case to be 'admissible', could aggravate the burden, for it could be that some less serious cases might consume its already limited time.

With the ending of the Cold War and the consequent increase in membership of Central and Eastern European democracies, the situation has been aggravated. With new applications still pending, the workload was set to grow immensely. Without reform, delays of up to ten years before a case reached fruition could have been a real possibility.

Because of this, some streamlining of the procedure was carried out, and under Protocol 8 the Commission is now permitted to sit in chambers of seven, or in some cases committees of three or more members who can carry out the initial sifting of cases which reach Strasbourg. Chambers conduct the investigation of cases where no new or difficult issue of principle is raised. Two chambers and six committees currently exist.

More radical proposals have been necessary, and for some time various proposals were in the air. Consideration was given to the idea of a merger between the Commission and the Court, and the abolition of some of the supervisory work of the Committee of Ministers. For a long while, Britain was seen by other member countries as obstructive in that it blocked any suggestions for change. However, at Vienna, in October 1993, changes were finally agreed. It was accepted that a single-tier Court, with fewer judges per case, sitting full-time, could reduce the delays. A new eleventh protocol to this effect was opened for signature in May 1994, and when ratification is completed by each member state, the new arrangements will apply. Currently, more than 30 states have now ratified the Protocol, and once Italy and Turkey have done so it will become effective.

The effect of the new arrangements

Each state will continue to have a single judge on the Court, and committees of three will screen cases to decide which ones fall outside of the jurisdiction of the machinery, or concern an issue on which the principle has already been decided. Chambers of seven will normally adjudicate on matters before the Court, but the then British Government insisted that, on exceptional issues which raise 'a serious question affecting the interpretation or application of the Convention', a 'grand chamber' of 17 judges should sit and deliver their verdict.

Even after the Vienna agreement was reached, Britain was seen by several of its partners as seeking to sabotage progress on streamlining the procedure. However, its attempt to hold up reform was outvoted by other states.

The fact is that the old procedure was a product of its era, a time when states were reluctant to hand over their sovereignty to an international court. It became a victim of its own success, and far-reaching change became necessary. As the Council of Europe continues to expand, with new members still expected from central and eastern Europe, the caseload is likely to continue to increase, perhaps at an even faster rate.

BRITAIN AND THE CONVENTION

Britain played a leading role in devising the Convention. It was drafted very largely by Sir David Maxwell-Fyfe, a member of the English Bar, later Attorney General and eventually a distinguished Conservative Lord Chancellor. Its language reflects much of English common law, and has echoes down the corridors of history, as far back as Magna Carta. On the continent, an early complaint was that the document was a very Anglo-Saxon one.

Britain was one of the original 15 countries to sign the Convention, and the first to ratify it in March 1951. The Labour government of 1965 gave British citizens the right of individual access to the machinery (Article 25), and subsequently this has been renewed every five years. It is due for ratification again in January 2001. However, although the Convention is binding on the British Government which may be forced to pay compensation, **it is not part of British law**. Citizens cannot gets its provisions enforced through the courts, because it has not been incorporated into the British system of justice. Many people who favour a bill of rights for Britain feel that rather than attempting to draw up a new one, on which agreement may be difficult to achieve, it would be easier to incorporate the

European convention into British law (see pp 92–5, for a fuller discussion of this proposal).

The British record at Strasbourg is a poor one. Few countries have experienced as many referrals to the Commission (in 1996 alone, there were 1,415) or had more cases declared admissible. Until 1992, Britain topped the league for adverse judgements in the European Court, a doubtful honour now assumed by Italy. By the end of 1995, Britain had had 80 cases adjudicated by the Court, in 37 of which at least one violation was found; in many of them compensation has been payable.

THE NEW HUMAN RIGHTS BUILDING, STRASBOURG. ESTABLISHED IN 1995, IT HOUSES ALL THE RELEVANT MACHINERY OF THE COUNCIL OF EUROPE

THE BRITISH RECORD AT STRASBOURG; A COMPARATIVE ANALYSIS

1   Cases registered as qualifying for examination of their 'admissibility' by the Commission (the worst five in 1989)

	1989	1992	1995
France	212	353	471
Germany (West to 1990)	169	137	223
Italy	142	196	554
Sweden	84	8	165
United Kingdom	224	222	413

2   Figures for Britain, 1996

Total number of Provisional Files	1415
Total number registered for test of admissibility	471
Total number registered as admissible	26
Total number of referrals to Government	77
Total declared inadmissible	305

3   Total number of Court cases involving violations to December 1995; the top 5 countries

Italy	85
Britain	37
Austria	35
France	34
Netherlands	21

Among many other cases concerning Britain, the Court has criticised treatment of suspected terrorists interned in Northern Ireland, allowed prisoners to correspond with their lawyers and others, upheld the rights of workers against closed shops, declared immigration rules to be discriminatory against women, ruled that the British government's ban on three British newspapers for disclosing evidence of MI5 wrongdoing in the *Spycatcher* case was invalid, restricted the power of the Home Secretary to lock up under-age killers, condemned the use of excessive force in the case of the shooting of IRA men by the SAS in Gibraltar, and secured the release of a Sikh leader who had spent six years in prison fighting deportation.

SOURCE: THE COUNCIL OF EUROPE

The first case concerning Britain was in 1975, when the Court ruled in favour of the right of a prisoner, Sidney Golder, to seek legal advice without the permission of the Home Secretary. There followed a succession of cases in which the rights of prisoners against the state were strengthened – including the right to marry, the right to send and receive letters uncensored and to sue prison officials for assault. Other types of cases involving Britain have included birching in the Isle of Man, the forcing of railway workers to join a trade union, ill-treatment of prisoners in Northern Ireland and several under the Prevention of Terrorism Act. Some have concerned the question of corporal punishment in schools, which is seen as degrading treatment. An example is given below.

Schoolboy Caning

In November 1992, the European Commission ruled that the caning of a former public schoolboy amounted to degrading treatment. He had been caned four times through his trousers, for defacing the cover of another child's file. His buttocks had been seriously bruised and swollen, and initially the police felt that there was evidence of assault causing actual bodily harm. The police had then dropped the matter, and in a civil action the judge said that the parents had implicitly permitted caning of their son in choosing the particular school that he attended.

By the settlement with the Commission, the British Government agreed to pay costs and £8,000 in compensation, though liability was not admitted. This stopped the case from going to the Court which would probably have ruled against Britain.

Recent British anxieties

Other countries in the Council have been keen to see Britain extend an unconditional right to its citizens to exercise the right of individual petition to the European Court. The Home Office and the Foreign Office have for some years taken a different view, the latter wanting to see Britain do as its partners wish, and the former taking the view that the system of five year renewal is a useful means of putting pressure on the Court.

The doubts entertained by the Home Office until 1997 were an indication of rising anxiety and irritation with some of the decisions of the Strasbourg machinery. A series of embarrassing rulings provoked further action, and in April 1996 a Foreign Office document was circulated to the other member states. It argued for governments to have the informal right to vet judges nominated by other countries. It also wanted states accused of violating the Convention to be given notice of impending controversy and the right to insist that more account by taken of differing democratic traditions in each country. A key passage was quoted in the *Guardian*:

Account should be taken of the fact that democratic institutions and tribunals in member states are best placed to determine moral and social issues in accordance with regional and national perceptions.

The Guardian 2.4.96

There was widespread dissatisfaction with the Court on the Right of the Conservative Party, stemming especially from the criticism issued (September 1995) of the SAS's killing of three IRA bombers in the Gibraltar shootings of 1987. Hints were dropped by some MPs that Britain should withdraw from the Convention, although others recognised that this would have been very embarrassing at a time when Britain was keen to promote democracy in the new states of central and eastern Europe, many of which had joined the Council or were contemplating doing so. A few Conservatives, even from the Right, felt that incorporation of the Convention into British law, might at least make British violations less high profile.

In November 1996, the British Lord Chancellor sought to persuade members of the European Court that change was needed, and there were some who were sympathetic to the need to create an independent judicial appointments commission. British ministers felt that the streamlining of the machinery under Protocol 9 presented an opportunity to curb the Court's powers. A more malleable body would certainly be more convenient to British ministers, but it would do little for the reputation of the Convention and those charged with enforcing it.

OTHER RIGHTS PROTECTED BY THE COUNCIL OF EUROPE

The Council has for several years examined ways of expanding the scope of its protection of human rights. It has done this by widening the range of the Convention, via the Protocols, but other initiatives have also been taken, such as introduction in 1965 of **The European Social Charter**, not to be confused with the Social Chapter of the European Union. The Charter – and an additional protocol – sets out a list of 23 fundamental social and economic rights and principles, tackling such topics as the right to work, the right to bargain collectively and to strike, and the right to social security and medical assistance. There is no enforcement machinery for this document.

In 1989, **The European Convention for the Prevention of Torture and Inhuman or Degrading Treatment or Punishment** came into being, and this provides additional safeguards for those detained in prison and elsewhere. A Committee is empowered to visit locations in which people are being detained and make recommendations for their better treatment. The visits are primarily to places where torture or other degrading treatment is suspected.

CONCLUSION

Britain has obligations under several pieces of international machinery. The Human Rights Committee can only report on British lapses; it cannot enforce its judgements. The institutions of the EU and the Council of Europe can make decisions which are binding in British law. Because of this, the issue of Parliamentary sovereignty has been raised by some politicians who worry about 'the European dimension'. Whatever the merits of the sovereignty question, the number of cases in which Britain has been 'in the dock' in Strasbourg is a cause for concern.

STUDY GUIDES

This section is designed to illustrate the nature and extent of Britain's current international obligations in the area of human rights. The reports of the UN Human Rights Committee provide useful examples of areas in which the British record is open to question. However, it is the European Union and the European Convention which are especially relevant, for we are bound by the decisions taken by the machinery involved.

Questions relating to the Convention are likely to concern its status in British law, and the merits of incorporation as a British bill of rights. For this, you need notes on the contents of the Convention, the means of enforcement and proposals for reform. Above all, ensure that you have an idea of the British record in Strasbourg.

If you are studying an option on European Government and politics, the work of the Council of Europe, particularly in the area of human rights, may be especially important.

Examination Hints

Use examples from this section to enrich your answers on the protection of rights in British Government and politics. Examiners are looking for up-to-date knowledge backed by appropriate comparative material. For instance, when discussing the case for and against a bill of rights (see Chapter 5), it is helpful if you are familiar with the approach adopted by those who devised the Convention, and particularly with the types of rights then considered to be important. If you are studying a European option or comparative government, then the information and data provided in this section should be invaluable in helping you to reach your own judgements.

Group Work

Each member of the group could be asked to produce a paper on one of the rights organisations to which Britain has obligations, outlining its development and assessing its usefulness in the protection of rights. For instance, the group might examine the contents of the European Convention as listed on pp 73–74, and its recent judgements. Members could be encouraged to reach conclusions as to the importance of the cases involved, and the merits of the findings. As regards Britain, they might contemplate some cases which have gone against Britain, and then assess why it is that the judgements of the Court have caused such an adverse reaction on the political Right.

SUMMARY: PROTECTION AVAILABLE UNDER THE UNITED NATIONS AND EUROPEAN UMBRELLAS (SIMPLIFIED VERSIONS)

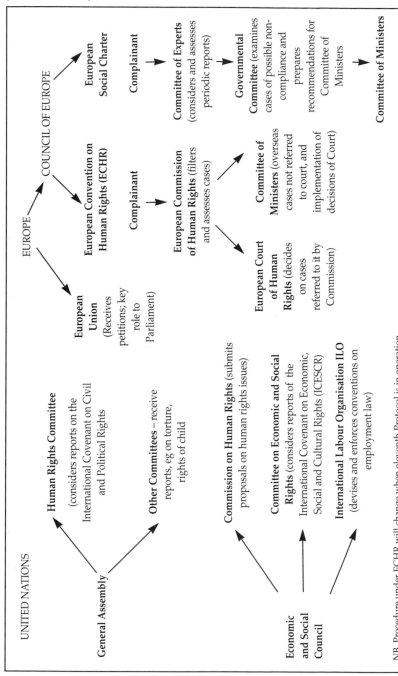

NB Procedure under ECHR will change when eleventh Protocol is in operation.

1 The European Convention has now been in existence for nearly 50 years. Account for its survival, and growing recognition.
2 Discuss the view that the machinery of the European Convention is in need of a considerable overhaul to make it more relevant to today's needs.

Glossary

Incorporation   Inclusion (eg of the European Convention into British law)

Just satisfaction   Financial compensation

Ratification   The act of giving formal approval

Violation   An infringement (eg of an agreement)

Further Reading and Resources

Cumper, P. (1996), 'The European Court of Human Rights,' *Talking Politics*, pp 43–6

E. Hooson. (1977), *The Case for a Bill of Rights*, distributed by the Liberal Party

McCrudden and Chambers, (1995), *Individual Rights and the Law in Britain*, the Law Society, Clarendon Press

Wallington, P. and McBride, J. (1976) *Civil Liberties and a Bill of Rights*, Cobden Trust pamphlet

Watts, D. *Politics Review*, April 1994, 'Europe's Bill of Rights', pp 149–51

5

A BILL OF RIGHTS FOR BRITAIN?

Introduction

BRITAIN HAS NO bill of rights, a legal document setting out and guaranteeing in law the basic liberties and entitlements of its citizens. Some observers believe that – given the absence of any written constitution – the individual is left without adequate protection for his or her rights. A government can dominate the House of Commons and use its majority to push through controversial measures which may limit essential freedoms.

Britain is now alone among the European democracies in lacking either a written constitution or an enforceable bill of rights, a constitutional code of human rights which is binding in law. For many people, the existing protection afforded to British citizens is now seen as inadequate, because of the extensive powers available to modern governments and other large institutions. The requirement is, in their opinion, for more effective legal remedies to safeguard the individual against their misuse.

Key Points
As you read this chapter, ask yourself:

- In what ways would incorporation of the ECHR advance the existing protection of rights in Britain?
- Is the protection afforded by the European Convention still adequate today?
- What would be the advantages in devising a wholly new bill of rights?
- Why is there so much suspicion of judicial power?
- How might the problems relating to Parliamentary sovereignty be overcome?
- Is a bill of rights of some sort the answer to the problem of the growth in executive power and the diminution of rights of recent decades?

THE GROWTH OF INTEREST IN A BILL OF RIGHTS

In recent decades, there has been growing support for the idea of a bill of rights which would list essential freedoms, ranging from freedom of association to freedom of expression, from freedom of conscience to freedom of the press. The Liberal Democrats have long been committed to the development of domestic rights legislation, and Labour has taken up the cause in the last few years. Their programmes include – but go beyond – the idea of incorporating the European Convention into British law. They view this as a desirable first step which is worthwhile in itself, but which needs to be followed by the adoption of other measures – most notably, the formulation of a home-grown British bill of rights. Liberal Democrats see this move as part of a wider plan which would include the adoption of a full written constitution.

Detailed proposals for such British bills have been advanced over several years, two of the most recent being the result of studies by the Institute for Public Policy and Research, and Liberty. The Freedom Association has long been committed also, but its provisions differ sharply from those of the other bodies (see below). Such suggestions draw heavily upon British experience of our international obligations under the Covenant and the Convention, but also upon the examples of legislation introduced in other countries. Indeed, it is notable that there is what the authors of *Human Rights Legislation* refer to as a 'cross-fertilisation of international human rights standards'. For instance, a leading Canadian judge, Justice Strayer of the Canadian Federal Court, was seconded to the Hong Kong Government to help its members devise their Bill of Rights Ordinance.

THE LIBERTY CHARTER OF CIVIL RIGHTS AND LIBERTIES

We are committed to the defence and extension of civil liberties in the United Kingdom and to the rights and freedoms recognised by international law. In particular, we are pledged to ensure and safeguard these essential rights:

1 To live in freedom and safe from personal harm.
2 To protection from ill-treatment or punishment that is inhuman or degrading.
3 To equality before the law and freedom from discrimination on such grounds as disability, political or other opinion, race, religion, sex, or sexual orientation.
4 To protection from arbitrary arrest and unnecessary detention; the right to a fair, speedy and public trial, to be presumed innocent until proved guilty, and to legal advice and representation.
5 To a fair hearing before any authority exercising power over the individual.
6 To freedom of thought, conscience and belief.
7 To freedom of speech and publication.
8 To freedom of peaceful assembly and association.

9 To move freely within one's country of residence and to leave and enter it without hindrance.

10 To privacy and the right of access to official information.

THE FREEDOM ASSOCIATION'S CHARTER OF RIGHTS AND LIBERTIES

We believe that in return for allegiance to the Sovereign in Parliament, citizens enjoy the rights to be governed according to the Rule of Law, duly enforced without fear or favour. We believe that the following rights and liberties belong to all and that they should be entrenched through a new constitutional settlement, for which the Association is pledged to work: amendment would thereafter be made only by affirmative vote through a referendum of the entire electorate, assented to by the Sovereign in Parliament.

1 The right to be defended against the country's enemies.
2 The right to live under the Queen's peace.
3 Freedom of movement.
4 Freedom of religion and worship.
5 Freedom of speech and publication.
6 Freedom of assembly and association for a lawful purpose.
7 Freedom to withdraw one's labour, other than contrary to the public safety.
8 Freedom to choose whether or not to be a member of a trade union or employer's association.
9 The right to own private ownership.
10 The right to dispose or convey property by deed or will.
11 Freedom to exercise choice or personal priority in spending, and freedom from oppressive, unnecessary or confiscatory taxation.
12 Freedom from all coercive monopolies.
13 Freedom to engage in private enterprise and pursue the trade or profession of one's choice without harassment.
14 Freedom of choice in the use of State and private services.
15 The right to protection from invasion of privacy.

THE CAMPAIGN FOR A BRITISH BILL OF RIGHTS

The campaign began to get under way in the late 1960s, and originally came from a range of individuals and groups across the political spectrum. Fabians of the political Left, Liberals in the Centre and some individual Conservatives on the Right began to be attracted to the idea. Quintin Hogg first put forward his ideas in a pamphlet '*New Charter*' in 1969. The House of Commons considered various bills from private members, and in that same year the Lords debated 'the need for protection of human rights and fundamental freedoms'. By the middle of the following decade, the matter had entered the realms of serious political debate, and in 1974 Lord Scarman took up the theme in his now famous Hamlyn lecture.

Two years later, the now-ennobled Quintin Hogg (Lord Hailsham) was arguing for a written constitution as well as a bill of rights in his *Dimbleby Lecture* for the BBC.

The restatement of Hailsham's views was an indication of the alarm then felt by some members of his party about its prospects of gaining power outright in the near future following a succession of disappointing election results. A bill of rights might at least make it unlikely that Labour would be in a position to put forward controversial legislation and force it through a reluctant Parliament. In *New Charter*, he wrote of his change of mind in this way:

> *I know, of course, that the traditional English view has been that remedies are more important than rights. Until recently, I agreed with this. I thought and I still think there was something in it...But ...the old remedies have proved inadequate in practice, and I fear that most of the modern prescriptions – even in our own party – do not go to the root of the matter.*
>
> *The nature of society has changed so much, that new tyrannies have risen – the trade unions, for instance, or vast commercial undertakings. The Ombudsman is not enough. There are far more cases of tyranny outside his jurisdiction than within it...It is the arbitrary rule of the modern Parliament itself which needs consideration. Every other country – including those Commonwealth countries – have insisted on safeguards of this kind, and in theory we are committed to it...the European Convention...is enforceable. Cannot our own judiciary be entrusted with some of the powers, which, at least in theory, we have entrusted to a European Court?*

The views expressed by such writers and speakers inspired much debate, both in Parliament and in articles in academic journals. In addition to a series of features by journalists, a number of eminent judges began to speak out on the issue as well, and in many cases their voices were added to those calling for a bill.

Whereas in the early days of the campaign, much of the sympathy for change came from sources on the Centre-Right, from the 1970s onwards – and especially in the 1980s – the initiative was coming from the Centre-Left. More radical politicians and thinkers were beginning to conclude that such was the danger of our traditional rights being eroded by the Thatcher administrations that it was necessary to provide some additional protection for our rights. Paddy Ashdown, speaking for the Liberal Democrats at the end of that decade, argued that 'a bill of rights is an essential, guaranteed and constitutional buttress for individual freedom, particularly in our centralised and unrepresentative political system'. As we shall see, Labour was not initially enthusiastic about this form of safeguard and preferred other methods of protection, but under the brief leadership of John Smith (1992–94), there was a change in its traditional outlook. His successor Tony Blair, significantly perhaps another lawyer, has embraced the idea of incorporation of the ECHR, and wishes to see this followed by the development of a domestic bill of rights.

INCORPORATING THE EUROPEAN CONVENTION INTO BRITISH LAW

The Convention is binding on the British Government which may be forced to pay compensation, but it is not part of British law. Citizens cannot get its provisions enforced through the courts, because it has not been incorporated into the British system of justice. Many people who favour a bill of rights for Britain feel that rather than attempting to draw up a new one, on which agreement may be difficult to achieve, it would be easier to incorporate the European Convention into British law. The Labour and Liberal Parties favour such a course, as do organisations active in the field of individual rights, such as Liberty.

If the Convention were incorporated and became the British bill of rights, then all British courts from magistrates' ones up to the House of Lords would have to interpret the law in accordance with the rights laid down in Strasbourg.

ARGUMENTS IN FAVOUR OF INCORPORATION

There are several arguments for a British bill of rights, support for which has grown in recent years. Charter 88 has been prominent in the campaign, and it wants a written constitution to enshrine traditional civil liberties. A number of judges and politicians, as well as those groups active in the campaign for stronger protection for our freedoms, have argued for such a bill.

Sometimes, the case is made in terms of the concentration of power in the hands of the executive, and its introduction of controversial laws for which the government has no overall popular support; others stress the threat to personal liberties which comes from the activities of the police or others in authority. On the Right, the emphasis is on the danger to freedom posed by a Labour government committed to public ownership and an extension of state control. On the Left, cases are mentioned where trade union rights or those of minority groups have been overridden.

However, the conflict between British law and certain international codes has added strength to the case. Since Britain ratified Article 25 of the Convention and became a member of the then European Community, we are at the mercy of European law.

The European Convention and Article 25 were originally ratified by Labour governments, and renewal has subsequently been done by Conservative ones, so that the document commands a fair degree of support. However, though it is available as a last resort, Conservative and Labour governments have been reluctant to go further and make it available for use in this country by aggrieved British citizens. To incorporate it in this way would have certain benefits, namely:

1　Britain would be more fully fulfilling its obligations under the Convention if we incorporated it, and the present anomalous status would be clarified. It is after all binding upon any British Government, and several cases have established that there are serious differences between European and British law – cases in which ultimately the Convention's finding is paramount. When a verdict is given against Britain, we have to amend the law to bring it into line with the Court's judgement.

2　British citizens could then get redress in Britain without having to go to Strasbourg, an experience which is time-consuming and can be expensive (sometimes costing £70,000 or more).

3　Most cases would not then need to reach the European Court, so that the 'dirty linen' of British injustice would not need to be washed in Strasbourg for all of Europe to behold. The European machinery would become only be a last resort for people who were still dissatisfied after going through the national procedures.

4　There would be a clear and positive statement of the rights of the citizen which would be a useful weapon in the armoury used to challenge the denial of rights. There would be a greater awareness of rights among British citizens. Furthermore, incorporation may have an educative impact on governments, legislators, prison warders, the police and others in authority, all of whom would see the need to ensure that their policies and actions were not likely to be found wanting by the courts.

5　At present, it is too easy for governments to 'play for time', in the knowledge that if they hold out for long enough the citizen might either 'give up' on the Strasbourg solution or that by the time of the Court's decision the issue will have lost its impact.

No-one would suggest that incorporation would remedy all ills and that injustice would never happen, but there would be a quicker and more effective way of remedying it than at present exists. Incorporation alone is not enough to protect rights, and specific anti-discriminatory legislation can still be employed to tackle abuses such as racial intolerance or low pay for women.

THE CASE AGAINST

Those who dislike the idea of incorporation echo many of the complaints about any bill of rights. They see it as unnecessary and feel that already there are ways of putting grievances right. In particular, they would stress the role of MPs in taking up complaints from their constituents, reinforced as they are by the Parliamentary Commissioner for some types of case.

Labour has traditionally feared that any bill of rights could be a check on some of the legislation its favours, such as nationalisation, compulsory purchase and the abolition of private schooling. It sees more value in a positive approach to rights, and in its 1990 Charter it proposed measures to guarantee individual liberty. It wanted to pass specific legislation to establish certain basic rights, some of which it claimed had been eroded over the Thatcher era.

Conservatives for the most part have also been unenthusiastic. Officially, the Party has shown little interest in the idea of incorporation. There have been individual voices calling for a bill or for incorporation, but these have been muted for some time. When there was last a Labour government, the voices were louder and more numerous.

In both cases, the parties have emphasised the sovereignty of Parliament, and believe that it is at Westminster that issues should be decided. It is up to Parliament to defend the people against injustice and to legislate for the type of society the government of the day favours. MPs are elected, and judges are not. Particularly in the Labour Party, there has been a great fear of judicial conservatism, and a belief that judges are more interested in preserving rights of property than in safeguarding the liberties of trade unions, or racial or other minority groups. A bill of rights would give them too much power to interpret the law in a restrictive way.

As for the Convention, its wording is often seen as vague and sweeping. Labour dislikes its approach on such matters as vagrancy and education. The Conservatives, especially on the Right, have been very uneasy about the number of cases in which their government has been defeated in Strasbourg, especially over matters such as the Prevention of Terrorism Act.

HOW INCORPORATION MIGHT COME ABOUT

Technically, incorporation is not difficult to achieve, but there are different ways by which it could be achieved. In countries which have a written constitution, the bill of rights usually has a special status, superior to ordinary legislation and less easily open to amendment. In Britain, there is no precedent for the notion of entrenching legislation, although the issue of entrenchment is not an necessarily an obstacle. Other countries have a tradition of Parliamentary sovereignty, in particular some of those in the Commonwealth, and this coexists alongside a rights document. In Britain, despite the preoccupation with and constant assertion of Parliamentary sovereignty, it has been long been acknowledged that the adherence to the Convention and to the European Union have seriously diminished it. Since joining the then European Community in 1973, the courts have been able to declare invalid existing and subsequent British legislation which is inconsistent with EC law. The decisions of the Court of Justice have shown that European law is superior to British legislation.

Certainly, any act of incorporation could be reversed in a future Parliament, so that in a sense it would not be permanently entrenched. Thus the nature of the relationship could be changed if Parliament so decided. But in the meanwhile, the ECHR would be superior to British laws. Usually, it will present no difficulty to interpret domestic laws in such a way that they comply with the Convention, and conflicts are likely to be few. If there is such a conflict, then the outcome would depend upon the way incorporation is brought about. The report of the Constitution Unit, *Human Rights Legislation*, offers three different but practical scenarios. The incorporating law could:

1   Say that when legislation cannot be interpreted consistently with the Convention, then domestic legislation will prevail – the New Zealand approach (a weak form of entrenchment).

2   Empower the courts not to give effect to existing legislation, and require that all subsequent legislation should be construed as consistent with the Convention, unless manifestly impossible – the Hong Kong solution (a stronger form), or:

3   Empower the courts not to give effect to existing and new legislation which is in conflict, unless Parliament says specifically that legislation will be applied 'notwithstanding' the inconsistency – the Canadian position (the strongest of the three options). The courts would not have the power to strike down an Act of Parliament which is intended by the House to override the ECHR.

The very strongest approach would be to say that all past and future laws must be in accord with the Convention. If there is a divergence, then British law and practice would be changed in all circumstances.

THE CASE FOR A HOME-GROWN BRITISH BILL OF RIGHTS

Any advocates of a British bill are likely to take the ECHR and rights conferred in other international treaties as the starting point for any discussion of further development of the protection required. Given the existing status of the ECHR which is legally binding following a Strasbourg judgement, its contents cannot be undermined by any new document. But some libertarian groups are dissatisfied with the Convention in its present form and would like to see additional rights included, the phraseology of others amended by qualifications, and a statement of rights which was more attuned to the British situation today than one drawn up a half century ago.

ARGUMENTS IN FAVOUR OF A BRITISH BILL

What is the case for starting again, notwithstanding the commitments undertaken already in connection with our existing obligations? It is argued that a new bill of rights could offer substantial benefits to the citizenry, and these we must now examine.

The starting point for any argument for a Bill is normally the existence in Britain of an over-powerful and centralised system of government. On election, any government is in a virtually unassailable position as long as it has a reasonable Parliamentary majority. This is the 'elective dictatorship' of which Lord Hailsham complained in his *Dimbleby Lecture*, a situation in which the scope of the executive branch has expanded so enormously, that it endangers rights which have evolved over centuries. At present, there appears to be no effective way of countering the trend, other than some means of buttressing individual and minority rights via a new document and/or written constitution.

In the light of this broad trend to ever-more-powerful executives, numerous benefits are said to follow from the introduction of a bill. These include the following.

1 That everyone would have greater confidence and a sense of personal assurance that their fundamental rights are enshrined by a clear statement of law. They would know that there is a document which they can quote should their rights be denied, hopefully having learned of their basic rights at school – just as young Americans are taught about the US Constitution and the first ten amendments to it. As a result of this increased knowledge and awareness, people would know of their entitlements, and be able to gain certain and speedy redress in the event of any abuse of their position. For minority groups, in particular, this would be a welcome safeguard.

2 That the government of the day and also Parliament, local councils and any other bodies which exercise power to make decisions which may affect people's lives, would be aware of the existence of such a document. It would have an important educative effect upon those who work in them, for they would be wary of producing bills or other decisions which trample on rights and may lead to contentious legal challenges. Lord Scarman has made the point that 'when times are abnormally alive with fear and prejudice, the common law is at a disadvantage; it cannot resist the will, however frightened and prejudiced it may be, of Parliament'. Because of this, those who legislate or who carry out legislation would be more concerned to anticipate, and thus avoid rules and actions which are harmful to individuals and groups.

Harold Laski, a left-wing academic and political thinker who served the Labour party in the early postwar era, explained the educative value well, in a pertinent observation on the proposal for a bill of rights:

Granted that the people are educated to the appreciation of their purpose, they serve to draw attention...to the fact that vigilance is essential in the realm of what Cromwell called fundamentals. Bills of rights are, quite undoubtedly, a check upon possible excess in the government of the day. They warn us that certain popular powers have had to be fought for, and may have to be fought for again. The solemnity they embody serves to set the people on their guard. It acts as a rallying point in the state for all who care deeply for the ideals of freedom.

3   That a Bill would assist the courts by providing an up-to-date statement of the legal position against which judges and juries could make and deliver their verdicts. This would enable them to act as more effective defenders of the rights of the citizen than is the case at present, when the status of the Convention is ambivalent, and the array of other relevant legislation is vast and in some cases unclear.

The example of the American Supreme Court over the Brown v Topeka Board of Education (1954) is often referred to in this context. There, the nine justices came down in favour of the individual (and ultimately of the vast racial minority which he represented) in their ruling that segregation was inherently unequal. It may have been some years before this landmark decision was followed up by legislation to ensure much greater equality of treatment, but nonetheless, few would dispute that the judgement made in the Warren Court was the major factor in promoting equal opportunities for black people. As a result, the Court can be seen as having acted as the guardian of their constitutional rights.

4   That a bill would not only establish the protection of rights from abuse by public authorities of the types mentioned, but also create a presumption that liberties should not be infringed by various powerful private groups and individuals, be they trade unions, large companies or religious cults.

In essence, then, the case is that the existence of a bill of rights drawn up for the era in which we live would re-emphasise the right of citizens against the state, rights which are always in danger of being whittled away. For those on the Left, the sort of actions against which people are seen as needing protection, lie mainly in the field of civil liberties. As we have seen, in too many situations, the position of minority groups and individuals has not been respected or defended. For those on the Right, the concerns are often different. The dangers perceived by rightwing writers centre more on the threat presented by the possible extension of an all-powerful socialist government which might override rights by showing too much concern for the position of trade unions and protesters, and too little for the property rights of sometimes wealthy citizens. From either standpoint or none, there are many people who feel that there is a need for a clear and contemporary statement of rights which can be quoted by any who feel that their feelings and needs are being ignored.

THE CASE AGAINST A BILL OF RIGHTS

For opponents of a bill of rights, there is a real doubt over whether such a document is necessary or likely to be effective in safeguarding rights than is done via the existing methods. Some – mostly today on the Right – believe that there is no problem, and that much of the alarm about an erosion of rights in the last couple of decades is unwarranted. Others accept that there is a problem. Indeed, they may see the state of our liberties as being in 'crisis', as do Ewing and Gearty. But they see little value in any declaration of rights, and believe that instead what is needed is a range of other measures (possibly even a change of culture) to rectify the alarming position in Britain today.

There are practical and theoretical doubts about the advantages to be gained from a bill of rights. An important practical consideration is the need to decide which rights would be protected. Presumably, the obvious ones are the First Amendment ones of the US Constitution, freedom of speech, of assembly and association among them. Such generalities might not prove controversial, but the difficulty arises when they are applied to particular circumstances. Rights are in most cases not absolute, and their relevance can vary according to the prevailing social and political climate. One person's right can conflict with the general needs of society. Social progress for the majority often involves a diminution of the rights of some individuals.

The rights claimed by Right and Left could vary significantly. Even the same term can be interpreted in different ways. Economic freedom is viewed differently on the two wings of the political spectrum. To those on the Right, it may be taken to refer to freedom from state interference, the liberation of individual initiative and allowing a person to do what seems to be in his or her best personal interests. A leftwinger might see the term as meaning freedom from poverty and unemployment, problems which may require government action to remedy them.

There is no ready-made consensus on basic rights, and this is especially true of the social and economic sphere. The legislation of one administration may be unacceptable to its political opponents who may feel that those injured by it are suffering a serious violation of their rights. Yet again, some rights might interfere with other ones. For instance, would the right of unions to develop a closed shop be protected? If such a claim was included, then future Parliaments would be bound by it. Yet in a subsequent Parliament, the overwhelming majority of MPs might be against this proposal and find it distasteful. But they would probably find themselves being forced to honour it, especially if the bill was entrenched.

Defenders of the present position tend to emphasise that Parliament is the main protector of our liberties. It is a fundamental part of the British Constitution that Parliament is a sovereign body, and that its elected representatives alone should make decisions relating to basic rights and any other matter. With a bill of rights, then on many disputed matters power would be taken from the hands of elected MPs and given to the judges.

Fears about the transfer of power to the judiciary are at the heart of anxiety about a bill of rights. Throughout much of its history, many in the Labour movement have felt that their party has suffered from the decisions made by those on the Bench, particularly in the area of industrial relations. The most famous example of such treatment was the Taff Vale case at the turn of the century, in which the right of the unions to take strike action was seriously restricted. In the 1980s, a number of sequestration cases were heard, in which union funds were taken away as a result of judicial decisions. These judgements, and several others, have served to fuel suspicion on the Left, a feeling which is deep-rooted among more traditional supporters of the Labour Party.

WHAT ARE THE GROUNDS FOR SUSPICION OF JUDGES?

Suspicion of judges has not arisen solely as a result of the unfavourable verdicts which they have often delivered. It has much to do with a feeling that these judgements derive from the backgrounds, attitudes and method of selection of those in the judiciary.

Firstly, many judges have reached their eminence having practised at the Bar, the membership of which has long been held to be elitist and unrepresentative. As a result of the manner of selection and the choice available, judges tend to derive from the professional middle classes, often having been educated at public school and then Oxbridge. They tend to be wealthy, conservative in their thinking and – like so many people in 'top' positions in British life – out of touch with the lives of people from different backgrounds.

A judge's generally privileged background does not, of course, render him or her necessarily biased in outlook, but critics would argue that the nature of their training and the character of the job which they undertake tends to give them a preference for traditional standards of behaviour, a respect for family and property, an emphasis on the importance of maintaining order and a distaste for minorities (especially if they are strident in their approach to seeking justice for their cause).

Given that a person's background should not disqualify him or her from getting on to the Bench (now less of an obstacle than was once the case), there is above all the problem of legitimacy. Appointment of judges is by the Prime Minister, and that itself opens the possibility that those appointed will be of a particular viewpoint. But it is the fact that they are *appointed* and therefore have no democratic mandate which causes particular concern. If there were to be a bill of rights, power would pass from elected politicians, who need to remain sensitive to the wishes of the voters, to unelected, unaccountable judges: from the representatives of the people to a group often criticised as being remote from present-day reality. Should it not be elected and accountable politicians who take policy decisions and resolve any conflicts of social and political values? Ewing and Gearty question whether it is:

> *legitimate or justifiable to have the final political decision, on say a woman's right to abortion, to be determined by a group of men appointed by the Prime Minister from a small and unrepresentative pool...Difficult ethical, social and political questions would be subject to judicial preference, rather than the shared or compromised community morality.*
>
> *Freedom under Thatcher, 1990*

Certainly, there is a danger of a politicisation of the judiciary which would become embroiled in the political arena as they sought to decide on the interpretation and/or validity of a particular piece of legislation. In the words of an opponent, Lord Lloyd:

> *To try to bring the judiciary into this sort of contest can only have one effect and that is to destroy the standing of the judiciary in the eyes of the people as a whole.*

To the argument that a bill of rights has been beneficial in the US in advancing the rights of black people and other individuals and groups, it could be countered that this is no guarantee that the same would apply in Britain with its different traditions. Moreover, the experience of the case often cited, Brown v the Topeka Board of Education, is less clear-cut than is often alleged. A different way of viewing the case is to point out that segregation was allowed to continue for so long before the 1954 judgement, and this with the approval of the Supreme Court which in 1896 had accepted that segregation was acceptable. Indeed, before that, as Ewing and Gearty remind us, the Court had decided that the Constitution did not apply to blacks.

There is a further consideration, related to the above point concerning the sovereignty of Parliament and the undesirability of giving a political role to judges. If it is the case that Parliament is currently unable to act effectively to maintain rights because of the tendency for the executive to acquire ever-increasing power, then there is a different solution to the creation of a bill of rights. This is to find other means of countering the trend, by such means as granting greater power to select committees and providing for the passage of a freedom of information act. Such measures could be taken before the any experimentation with a bill of rights and/or written constitution, and would not involve the threat to Parliament's sovereignty which so alarms critics of the bill.

SOME CURRENT PROPOSALS FOR A BILL OF RIGHTS

Various proposals have been put forward for some kind of charter of our liberties and rights. These include the ones put forward by the Institute of Economic Affairs and by the Freedom Association, both of which are rightwing bodies whose documents would have sought to preserve property rights and safeguard the country from excesses of trade union power.

THE CHARTER 88 CONVENTION IN NOVEMBER 1991 IN PROGRESS (TIM MILLER, BEVERLY ANDERSON AND ANTHONY BARNETT SHOWN)

An attempt to work out the implications of any such bill and to deal with the difficulties which their introduction may raise was made at a convention held in November 1991, organised by Charter 88. Various campaigners came together to seek to establish a consensus between organisations committed to greater protection. A number of proposals were examined, including those from the Institute for Economic Affairs, and the Institute for Public Policy Research (IPPR). The position of the judges was a key issue in the discussion.

THE IPPR PROPOSAL

The version drafted in 1990 by the left-leaning think-tank, the IPPR, was a detailed one, based substantially on both the European Convention and the

United Nations Covenant. It attempted to deal with this by proposing reforms in the selection and training of judges, so that the Left might find the personnel and outlook of the judiciary more acceptable. A new judicial appointments commission of legal and lay representatives would be charged with the task of tackling the problems of gender and racial imbalance. A reformed judiciary might then help to create 'a culture in which the protection of rights is central to our law, where people know their rights and can claim them'.

THE LIBERTY PROPOSAL

The distinctive feature of the Liberty proposal (1991), *A People's Charter*, Liberty's bill of rights, again concerned the position of the judges in any new arrangement. They were not to have the final day in matters of rights, bearing in mind that in the eyes of civil libertarians they have too often failed to mount a sufficient challenge to the power of the executive. By their approach, members of Liberty hoped to gather support from all those who wanted to see rights better protected, but were anxious about any increase in judicial power. They took the view that any bill of rights should not be so far entrenched that the rights protected could not be changed by the democratic process – they disliked the American example, where amendment is hard to achieve.

In borderline cases, where someone has to decide on the political meaning of the text and which rights should prevail, the matter should be referred to a scrutiny committee of the House of Commons which would be given the power to over-ride the judge if two-thirds of its membership so wished. In such cases, the judicial role would be confined to the interpretation of the legal issues involved, and Parliament's ultimate supremacy would be acknowledged. A reformed Second Chamber would be empowered to delay for five years the enactment of any legislation that expressly violated the bill of rights, and this idea – with which Labour has toyed in recent years – would represent a further strengthening of the position of Westminster under the new arrangements.

The Liberty document is a lengthy one (118 pages), and there is amplification about what is meant by each right. The 'right to life' is not left open to interpretation according to the particular circumstances of the case. It is instead made specific, so that the death penalty for piracy or treason would be repealed, and abortion still permitted.

The Liberty charter is skilfully constructed. It confronts the fears of the sceptics and avoids the pitfalls into which some other countries have fallen. The proposals are necessarily untried, but have parallels in current practice. The

European Convention is enforced by the Committee of Ministers as well as by the Court, and there several similarities with the Canadian document. If something akin to the proposal were to be adopted, along with the reform of the judicial system which Liberty – like the IPPR – favours, then it may be that many of the reservations of those opposed to a bill of rights would be overcome.

DIFFERING ATTITUDES TO JUDGES: THE ACADEMIC CRITIQUE
(SEE ALSO PP 29, 99–100, 117, 122–23.)

A bill of rights, whether based on the European Convention or otherwise, would effectively bestow substantial powers upon those charged with interpreting it. Many of those who oppose such a document express strong reservations about the suitability of judges to operate fairly in this area.

British Judges ...

British judges were once regarded as persons of integrity, incorruptible men and women of honour and merit. Lord Justice Hewart expressed recognition of this high regard, when he observed back in 1936 that: 'Her Majesty's judges are satisfied with the almost universal admiration in which they are held'. Today, such a view seems breathtakingly complacent. Public perception now falls far below that assumed by Hewart. A succession of cases in which miscarriages of justice have occurred and the judiciary was conspicuously reluctant to question its own earlier judgements have raised doubts. So too has the tendency of some judges to make insensitive observations when handling cases affecting class, gender and race. In rape cases especially, some highly inappropriate observations have been made. Such occurrences help to create the impression that attitudes from a different world to that inhabited by the majority of people prevail among the judiciary.

and their critics

Academic critics have been more precise in expressing their concerns. R.M. Jackson has questioned the notion of an 'impartial' judge, and observes that:

Strong views may obviously affect decisions, but general outlook and mental habits can have just as much influence without being so noticeable. Whatever the conscious effort to be impartial, and here our judges have had a high standard, there is always the 'prejudice' or 'bias' or as Holmes called it the 'inarticulate premiss' of the Judge.

A leftwing critic, **Professor J.A.G. Griffiths**, has similarly expressed serious doubts as to whether the judiciary could ever be impartial. In a modern society, he sees them as an essential part of the system of government, charged with the task of upholding the values of British life and resisting the attempts of those who would wish to transform them: 'Judges are part of the machinery of authority within the state and as such cannot avoid the making of political decisions'. They have a particular view of the national interest and in issues where there is a dispute between the state and citizen are more likely to side with the Executive than with striking miners, militant unions, leak-prone civil servants or minority activists. In his words:

We must expect judges, as part of that authority to act in the interests, as they see them, of the social order. The judges define the public interest, inevitably from the viewpoint of their own class...Those values are the maintenance of law and order, the protection of private property, the containment of the trade union movement, and the continuance of governments which conduct their business largely in private and on the advice of what I have called the governing group.

Lord Denning observed in one security case brought under the old OSA that:

When the state is in danger, our own cherished freedoms and even the rules of natural justice have to take second place'. Griffiths, has noted that men such as Denning have often allowed the judicial system to be bent 'to the needs of the politicians', and that sometimes 'the principles of the rule of law have been sacrificed to the expediency of the political and economic situation.

The question arises: if judges are prone to the failings which such critics have discerned, are they then the people best suited to pronounce on issues involving libertarian considerations? Griffiths notes their poor record in upholding specifically civil libertarian legislation, and in particular how they have tended to minimise the effects of the Race Relations Acts by adopting a narrow and unhelpful interpretation of the statutes.

Ralph Miliband, a Marxist, has been even more dismissive of the approach adopted by judges. He argues that in a capitalist country the whole legal system is class-based. Judges are part of the political structure, and share its assumptions. They seek to protect private property and the profits of a minority ruling class.

From a very different (and more rightwing) perspective, **Professor Philip Norton** takes a diffferent line. In his view, whatever the backgrounds from which they are drawn, their competence or their capriciousness in adjudication, there is a more fundamental objection to allowing reliance on judges to interpret any bill of rights and thereby becoming involved in political questions. This is that it is Parliament, comprising the elected MPs, which should decide whether abortion or capital punishment is permissible, what the age of consent should be, and other controversial questions. He quotes Lord Lloyd in the 1986 *McCluskey Lecture*, who observed:

The fact of the matter is...that the law cannot be a substitute for politics. The political decisions must be be taken by politicians. In a society like ours, that means by people who are removable.

Reform or bill of rights?

For some the criticisms relating to the backgrounds, past behaviour and role of judges are overwhelming objections to the introduction of a bill of rights. Of course, even if much of the academic critique is accepted, this could be seen as a strong argument for reform of the judiciary rather than an overwhelming objection to a bill of rights. Moreover, some judges have in recent years shown a greater willingness to stand up for individual rights and toinvoke 'European' considerations when presiding over their courts.

THE ATTITUDES OF POLITICAL PARTIES TO INCORPORATION AND A BILL OF RIGHTS

THE CONSERVATIVE PARTY

The official Conservative Party has shown little interest in a bill of rights. Supporters of the idea such as Lord Hailsham went notably quiet after 1979, his worries about an 'elective dictatorship' seemingly being more acute when a Labour government was in power. As for Incorporation of the European Convention into British law, there have been a very few MPs who are sympathetic although the majority are currently ill-disposed to much European machinery. Many of the decisions of the Court during the years of Tory rule were disliked by the Parliamentary party, for they seemed to confirm that anything that derived from Europe was suspect and probably not in British interests. Individual voices have been heard in favour of incorporation, if only to stop the embarrassing series of cases in which British 'dirty linen' has been available for all to see in Strasbourg.

THE LABOUR PARTY

For many years, Labour showed a notable lack of commitment on issues of constitutional reform. This was surprising for a party which was interested in the provision of minority rights, and which had legislated to add to those available by the Equal Pay Act, the Sex Discrimination Act and the Race Relations legislation. A commonly-held view was that a bill of rights was unnecessary, given the other measures of protection available, particularly through Parliament. Moreover, such a document might actually serve to stifle progress in securing basic liberties. In this feeling, they were perhaps encouraged by a remark of Lord Hailsham in the days when Labour was in power. He argued that 'the present government...is persistently proposing legislation...which would almost certainly be caught' by a Bill.

The Labour approach was to point out that a bill of rights represented a negative approach to freedom, whereas it wanted to see positive government action to promote equality before the law, give minorities more rights and provide more open government. It was wary of the European Convention too, for this was thought to be deficient in several respects. At a time when some party thinkers still favoured the abolition of private education, they could have found that this aspiration fell foul Article 2 of the first Protocol, which asserted not only the right to education, but also the 'right of parents to ensure that such education and teaching are in conformity with their own religious and philosophical convictions'.

Roy Hattersley, the Shadow Home Affairs spokesmen prior to 1992 election, was the person responsible for chairing the Policy Review Group which considered the protection of rights following the 1987 election defeat. His initial comments' reported in the Guardian in December 1988, reflected many of his and the party's long-standing suspicions about the Convention;

> *We know that the European Convention on Human Rights – the model for a written constitution which is most commonly canvassed for incorporation into British law – is claimed by the public school pressure groups as protection for their privileged status. No-one even suggests that it enshrines the right of every boy and girl to receive an education suitable to age, aptitude and ability. It simply asserts that 'no person shall be denied the right to education'. That means that the state shall not prevent a child from going to school. But prevention (as it would be defined by the courts) is not the problem. The problem is the state's failure to enable all children to attend schools which meet their needs. Focusing attention on the negative view of freedom – freedom from unreasonable state interference – is not enough. A constitution based on that principle protects those who already enjoy an acceptable standard of living. It often deflects attention from those who do not. By their nature, written constitutions ignore – and therefore diminish – the importance of positive freedom.*

By June 1991, when discussion of our constitutional arrangements had become a much more 'live' issue for debate, his position had moved. He was reported in the same newspaper as seeing some value in a bill of rights which set out general principles, but which would exist side by side with specific legislation which dealt with particular freedoms. He was still unattracted by the Convention, whose

> *principles are so general that they are often meaningless and are then almost qualified out of existence by sub clauses that try to make the principles a practical legal prospect.*

His 'conversion' to some form of Bill – though not to the European Convention – had been brought about by three 'increasingly attractive' arguments which he had come to appreciate:

1 support would be a demonstration of Labour's sincere commitment to the cause of protecting citizens' rights:
2 such a bill might help to create the climate of opinion in which to legislate for more individual rights, and;
3 a bill might fill in some of the gaps, and offer protection for freedoms and entitlements not already covered by specific legislation.

He had come to accept that what might 'loosely be called a bill of rights' could be useful as a statement of general principle. He recognised the popularity of the term, for it was one with which people could easily identify. Expressed in a general way, it would not conflict with Labour's more detailed proposals. The specific legislation would have priority, but the framework document 'would guide and govern the courts where, and only where, the specific law as silent'.

After the election defeat in 1992, John Smith, the new leader, showed more enthusiasm for a bill of rights and pledged himself to examine the case for incorporation of the ECHR. He subsequently addressed Charter 88, and committed himself to a bill of rights, and saw incorporation as an essential step in this direction.

THE LIBERAL DEMOCRAT PARTY

As for the Liberal Democrat Party, it has long favoured measures to promote individual rights. Members pride themselves on their clear commitment, and see the issue as one which is especially their own. The term 'Liberal' implies a belief in individual liberty, and the rights of the citizen (they use the word citizen a great deal, a significant point because unlike a subject a citizen has rights) and the protection of minorities fits in with the general party philosophy. They portray the Conservatives as being only concerned with the freedom of the market place, with a definition of liberty which is narrowly confined to the economic sphere and even there concentrates only on providing opportunities for the most powerful in society. Labour is seen as locked into an old-fashioned belief in the importance of collective rights over individual ones, the union or class taking precedence over the individual.

For Liberals then, the right of each person to develop and express his or her talents is not a marginal issue but one at the heart of the political debate. Rights are not seen as negotiable, and given such instincts it is not surprising that they are fully committed to incorporation and to then moving forward to the provision of a written constitution. Liberals also advocate a British commission of human rights to assist complainants in bringing proceedings under the bill of rights, to secure compliance with its provisions, to review law and practice in the sphere of civil liberties and to recommend changes in existing law and practice.

CURRENT INTENTIONS AND FUTURE PROSPECTS

It is of course the Labour Party which is in a position to take up the issue. It held pre-election talks with the Liberal Democrats which led to agreement on the programme for introducing measures of constitutional reform, and in its *1997 Manifesto* included a strong section on 'real rights for citizens'. Pledged to a statute to incorporate the European Convention and to other measures on the subject, it seemed likely that – once in office with a powerful majority – there would be early progress along the lines outlined below.

In October 1997, the government published a White Paper entitled 'Bringing British Rights Home'. It indicated that the Human Rights Bill will incorporate the European Convention into British law, so that for the first time a declaration of fundamental human rights will be enshrined into British Law. The detail in the proposals reveals that ministers have decided not to empower the courts to strike down offending Acts of Parliament, as happens in Canada. Instead, judges will be able to declare that the law is incompatible with the Convention, and this 'will almost certainly prompt the Government and Parliament to change the law'.

Civil rights campaigners had feared that Labour would go for the weaker, New Zealand form of incorporation. They welcomed the right of judges to make a formal declaration of incompatibility and the introduction of a fast-track process to amend offending laws swiftly. They also noted that in future, ministers must certify that any new law complies with the Convention. Some lamented the absence of Human Rights Commission, although the door is left open to the creation of such a body. Discussions will take place with the Community Relations and Equal Opportunities Commissions on the desirability of such an innovation, and a committee of both Houses of Parliament will advise the Home Secretary on whether there should be one all-embracing Commission.

The approach adopted will transform relationships between the executive, Parliament, the judiciary and the citizen. It will signal a substantial shift in the balance of constitutional power between Parliament and the judiciary, with judges gaining the powers to overrule governmental decisions if they breach fundamental rights. Some Conservatives – including the Shadow Home Secretary at the time of writing, Dr Mawhinney – have denounced the proposals as a clear erosion of Parliamentary sovereignty. They are likely to quote the observation of the current Lord Chancellor, Lord Irvine, who has admitted they involve 'a very significant transfer of power to judges'.

The argument that democracy will be the loser if powers are handed over to the judiciary does carry more weight by virtue of the current nature of the composition of the Bench, for we have a situation in which there is neither a woman or member of the black or Asian minority presently sitting. The case for moves to reform the method of appointing judges is a strong one, as the IPPR has pointed out. Its members are still predominantly white, male, middle class and conservative, and the widening of its social base has been noticeably slow in comparison with some other professions. But the context in which they work has already changed over the last two decades, and an awareness of their role in policing the activities of government has become much more widespread. Moreover, if judges have often in the past seemed to be the slaves of the executive and of British conservatism, this might be because they have operated in a non-rights based order. Given a situation where rights are emphasised more than ever before, they may well accommodate to the new thinking.

Labour is likely to reject the charge that incorporation is a further step along the road to Euro-domination of our constitutional arrangements, by pointing out that rather than importing an alien body of European legislation what it is really doing is repatriating British legislation given to the continent shortly after the Second World War. The Convention was, after all, largely a British creation, and when it was drawn up the labour Lord Chancellor of the day assumed that incorporation would be automatic. It has been a slow journey for Labour to return to its original position. For much of the intervening period, the party has recoiled from European commitments and been wary of the idea of judicial power. With its recent determination to bring about a more rights-based culture, it has come to accept that the political significance of judges has increased, is increasing and will not be diminished.

CONCLUSION

A bill of rights is not a panacea for all problems which arise in the relationship between the individual and the state. Neither incorporation of the ECHR nor the development of an entirely new British document would prevent the misuse of power by those in authority, and history is littered with examples of countries in which formal statements of rights have not proved to be worth the paper upon which they were recorded.

On the one hand, we have the experience of communist China, whose constitutional guarantees of freedom did not prevent the massacre in Tiananmen Square in 1989. If it is thought that a totalitarian example is unfair, then India in the early 1970s (where the ruling Mrs Gandhi declared a sudden state of emergency and arrested opposition leaders) provides an example of a democracy where constitutional provisions were not respected. The existence of the US Bill of Rights did not stop President Franklin Roosevelt from depriving thousands of native-born Japanese Americans of their liberty in the Second World War, whilst for generations the Bill did not apply to American blacks. It remains the case that if a political system operates to protect human rights, it has more to do with the attitudes and political culture of its society than with the formalities of any declaration.

For a long while, the traditional view of British governments has been that:

* We have no need to incorporate the Convention because compliance can be achieved already without it, and
* it is a fallacy to assume that single codified documents automatically best protect individual rights.

These views were restated by John Patten in his writing on political culture:

> *Such documents are meaningless unless they exist within a country which has a political culture that renders them viable ... The greatest protector of citizens' rights in the UK are citizens themselves ... The protector of freedom in the end is the political culture, not some document, however weighty.*
>
> CPC lecture, July 1991

Jeremy Bentham, a political thinker of the early nineteenth century, would have agreed. He dismissed the Declaration of the Rights of Man as a piece of 'nonsense on stilts'. Since then, many others have been similarly dismissive of such documents as either too abstract or too detailed to be of concrete value. Yet there is a long history of support for this approach, and in the debates over the American constitution Thomas Jefferson could not understand why anyone should resist the idea. As he put it:

> *A Bill of Rights is what the people are entitled to against every government on earth, general or particular, and what no just government should refuse or rest on inference.*

Since then, many who have wished to strengthen individual and minority rights in relation to growing state power have seen some kind of bill of rights as the best means of achieving such a change.

Table 7: *Summary: a bill of rights for Britain?*	
In favour	**Against**
1 People would have a clearer idea of their rights and duties under the rule of law, and courts would be clearer on the law to be enforced.	Rights are already adequately protected via Dicey's 'three pillars'. In addition, the Ombudsman, media and pressure groups are useful avenues for redress.
2 Liberties are better protected by the courts than under a majority government in a sovereign Parliament (elective dictatorship).	Parliament is better than the courts in dealing with what are often highly 'political' issues such as industrial relations, employment law etc. MPs, moreover, are elected and accountable, unlike judges.
3 Rights are increasingly under threat, and in last two decades the emphasis on law and order has damaged liberty.	Difficulty in agreeing on content and status of any bill. Especially over economic and social rights, there is conflict – just as there is over the degree of firmness of entrenchment.

4 A bill would have educational value and help promote a 'culture of rights' in which people are vigilant in defending freedom, and the behaviour of those in authority is restrained.	Written documents which reflect the climate of opinion at the time of their adoption can be inflexible – eg, US gun control provisions.
5 The example of the European machinery is encouraging. Under the ECHR, many rights have been secured.	Overseas experience not always encouraging (see point 4), and anyway culture/traditions differ around the globe
6 Such bills work well in other countries. In the USA, the Supreme Court has been an independent guardian of the Constitution and rights, eg, 1954.	If necessary, other measures can be introduced, such as Freedom of Information (FoI) legislation. These do not threaten Parliamentary sovereignty.

STUDY GUIDES

Revision Hints

This is a key chapter. You are likely to be asked about the case for and against a British bill of rights, or at least of incorporating the European Convention. You know what is in the Convention from Chapter 4. List the advantages and disadvantages of incorporating it into British law. Write a paragraph on the difficulties this might pose, and another on how it might/will be done.

As for a home-grown bill of rights, examine the two proposals given on pp 102–03 and mentally note the differences in their contents. Write a paragraph each on

1   the difficulties in devising a new bill;
2   the necessity for a bill and
3   the case against it.

Summarise the main reasons why Conservatives do not want such a bill, and why the Labour Party and the Liberal Democrats favour action. You should ensure that you understand the evolution in Labour's thought.

Examination Hints

You are likely to be asked one of three questions on this topic. You could get a general question on the need for a bill of rights or for incorporating the European Convention. Alternatively, you may be asked about the role of the judiciary under any new arrangements, or about the position of the Labour (or just possibly the Conservative) Party on the issue.

Note the importance of key words, as in the question: Should Britain *entrench* a bill of rights? Not only are you asked to express an opinion, but the word entrench needs to be tackled. In other words, what should the status of a bill be?

In talking about the role of judges, it is important to understand why Labour is wary of their key influence in adjudicating on rights issues. How effectively do the IPPR/Liberty proposals meet Labour's anxieties? Is Parliamentary sovereignty a problem? Could it be overcome by the Liberty approach? Or is it better to opt for the type of bill over which Parliament has ultimate control?

Group Work

This is a good topic for a class debate, along the lines that: 'A British bill of rights is essential to protect the liberties of the individual at a time when governmental power continues to increase'.

A useful exercise is to compare the rights contained in the European Convention (see Chapter 4), with those in the Freedom and Liberty charters. Members could be asked to pick out the features of each which they most admire. They might consider in what ways an incorporated Convention is inadequate to meet the need for full protection in today's world.

Practice Questions

1 Why does Britain not have a modern bill of rights?
2 Does Britain need an entrenched bill of rights?
3 Is it true to say that the primary reason for demanding a bill of rights in Britain is the inadequacy of existing Parliamentary protection for civil liberties?
4 Should the judiciary be more involved in resolving issues of civil liberties?
5 'It will be too difficult to achieve agreement on a new bill of rights for Britain. It is easier to incorporate the European Convention and call this the modern British bill of rights'. Discuss.
6 Examine the changing outlook of the Labour Party on the best means of protecting essential freedoms in Britain.

Glossary

Entrenchment   Establishment (firm or otherwise); a strongly entrenched bill is unamendable other than by some extraordinary process

Incorporation   Inclusion (eg, of European Convention in British law)

Parliamentary sovereignty   The idea that Parliament is the supreme law-making body, and that no Parliament can bind its successors

Political culture More than merely public opinion, but such features as the idea of the freeborn Englishman, the weight of history and the traditional British way of doing things

Totalitarian regimes Regimes in which the power and influence of the state is all-pervasive, and the position of the individual considered to be subservient – eg communist countries

Further Reading and Resources

Ewing and Gearty, (1990) *Freedom under Thatcher*, Clarendon Press

Griffith, J.A.G., (1991) *The Politics of the Judiciary*, Fontana

Jackson, R.M. (1972) *The Machinery of Justice in England*, Cambridge University Press

McCrudden and Chambers, (1995) *Individual Rights and the Law in Britain*, Oxford University Press

Norton, P., *Talking Politics*, Summer 1993, 'The case against a bill of rights'

Patten, J., CPC Lecture, July 1991, *Political Culture, Conservatism and Rolling Constitutional Changes*

Robertson, G., (1994) *Freedom, the Individual and the Law*, Penguin

Human Rights Legislation, 1996, Constitution Unit (briefing papers)

6

CONCLUSION

THERE HAS BEEN growing interest in British constitutional reform in recent years. Several areas of government activity have been the subject of searching enquiry and have been found wanting. From the introduction of the Parliamentary Commissioner for Administration in 1967 (and later of other 'ombudsmen' for health and local councils), change has been on the agenda. More recent suggestions – electoral reform, Lords' reform, devolution to Scottish and Welsh assemblies and possibly to regional authorities, and the introduction of a Freedom of Information Act – are all in some way concerned with providing rights for a section of the population. But specifically, in the last 20 years, there has been an increasing consideration of the idea of a written constitution as existing in other European democracies, and/or a bill of rights, as the best means of ensuring that civil liberties and rights are better protected.

Britain is alone in failing to incorporate the European Convention into British law, so as to provide adequate and effective remedies for alleged breaches of Convention rights and freedoms. This means that people in France, Germany, Italy, the Netherlands and elsewhere have remedies for the misuse of state power which are denied to British citizens. They have had to seek redress for human rights violations in Strasbourg, via the European Commission and Court, because Parliament has not authorised our court to provide remedies in Britain. The result, as we have seen, is that Britain has an unenviable record, with more referrals and breaches of the Convention than almost any other state.

A CRISIS IN BRITISH CIVIL LIBERTIES?

Ewing and Gearty have sensed a crisis in civil liberties in recent years, which demands immediate remedial action. They do not claim that this alarming situation was created by deliberate malevolence, but rather that Margaret Thatcher was able to make full use of the scope for untrammelled power which has always existed in the British Constitution, but which has been obscured by the scruples of earlier, more consensus-based politicians. Dworkin made a similar point, seeing Thatcherism's challenge to freedom as arising not so much from any despotic inclinations, but more from a mundane insensitivity to the importance of personal liberty.

A series of polls have also highlighted growing anxiety about the erosion of democracy and civil liberties, notably the *State of the Nation* conducted under the auspices of the Rowntree Trust. The 1995 one revealed increasing support for a domestic bill of rights, with 79% indicating their agreement that British people needed greater protection. However, it is worth recalling the words of Lord Lloyd who remarked that apart from when pollsters ask them questions on the subject, the reaction of many individuals to matters of rights was hardly one of deep concern. Speaking of the publication of the Lords' Report, he noted that:

> *so far as the public and the Press were concerned, [it] was received with practically a deafening silence. We did in fact hold a Press conference on the day the report appeared and I am sorry to have to tell your Lordships that only one representative of the Press turned up.*

THE ROOT OF THE PROBLEM A GROWTH OF CENTRAL POWER?

There has been a widespread belief among academics and commentators that the basis of our rights is at present inadequate. They range in their concern from the anxious to the alarmed, a common anxiety being the increase in the strength of the executive branch over the last couple of decades, or more. Executive power has sometimes been ruthlessly deployed, in a way careless of the rights of individuals. Dworkin, Ewing and Gearty and others have been foremost in pinpointing the dangers, much of their illustrative evidence deriving from the Thatcher era. During that time, the government increased state power more than ever. Uncontrolled by the supreme law of a written constitution, unlimited by an enforceable bill of rights, always enjoying a commanding majority in the House of Commons, the then administration extended the powers of the central state, eroding traditional checks and balances at the expense of civil and political rights.

This view of government as all-powerful and unchecked by the traditional checks and balances identified by Dicey, has been questioned by some critics of the proposal for a bill of rights. In particular, Professor Norton has pointed to the fragmentation as much as to the centralisation of the British political scene. He refers to new sources of power such as the European dimension, and in particular stresses the plurality of British politics, with the number of pressure groups having mushroomed in the past generation. Noting that we are a more 'rights-conscious' society today, he believes that groups enable many people to do something about the pursuit of their rights in a way impossible back in the 1950s and early 1960s. He refers to 'a burgeoning of groups determined to effect a change in the law to protect particular individuals and minorities in society', and argues that their willingness to challenge the actions of government means that ministers now operate in an environment in which they are 'more constrained by a growth of bodies enjoying political clout'.

The Norton view that the fear of an elective dictatorship is overstated has received some backing from others commenting on the dangers it poses for freedom in this country. In a House of Commons debate in 1987, Fred Silvester MP expressed it in this way:

> *It is a curious argument that we should adopt a radical change in our Constitution on the hypothesis that evil may come, but without any evidence that it has. The elective dictatorship could only come about if all the existing institutions that preserve our freedoms suddenly collapsed about us. However, I see no evidence of that.*

Different people come to different conclusions about the drift to central power, and those alarmed by the threat have divergent views as to what should be done. Some wish to see consideration of electoral reform, believing that this might bring about a genuine shift away from government dominance of Parliamentary life. Others, such as Dworkin, want a bill of rights, or at the very least, the incorporation of the Convention into British law. Electoral reform might lead to a revision of the way in which power is exercised. Such a democratisation of power might ensure that there is an extension of rights. Dworkin, and others, would argue that a clear proclamation of rights would democratise power.

THE SOLUTION: A BILL OF RIGHTS OR OTHER MEASURES?

Support for a bill of rights

Those alarmed at the erosion of liberties in recent decades often argue that a bill of rights – whether it be an incorporated Convention in the short term, or a home-grown version produced over a longer period – would provide a bedrock upon which future legislation could be based. It would demonstrate that individual freedom is seen as worthy of greater protection than is currently available, and would have an important educational influence on governments, Parliament and the judiciary. People would have a document which they could cite, when their rights are under threat and possess a means of speedy redress in the British Courts.

The existence of such a proclamation – if we get one in any form – should not induce complacency about our liberties, but could be a useful part of a 'rights package'. To others, worried about the growth in importance of the unelected judges, supporters of the bill respond that a statement of rights might diminish the judges' actual influence, even if it would increase their formal power For them, rights do not belong to judges or to the courts. They belong to the people, and especially to minorities and to the oppressed. A political culture in which people feel they have rights and can claim them, is by this fact alone more democratic than Britain's. The key point about rights, therefore, is not that they increase the power of judges but that they increase the power of ordinary people.

Opposition to a bill of rights

Opponents of a bill of rights are unconvinced. They fear that written rights will mean more power for those who have it already, particularly members of the judiciary. Ewing and Gearty in *Freedom under Thatcher* quote copious examples to show that even where courts have already assumed the application of the European Convention, they have often used it to justify rulings against the individual and in favour of the executive. Theirs' is a formidable indictment of the Bench, and it goes a long way to explain why Labour was so slow to move towards its present support for a bill of rights.

Sceptics such as Ewing and Gearty see the proposal for a bill of rights as too glib to tackle the current situation. They doubt any move supported so strongly by the legal profession, and sense that there is an element of self-interest. Such a bill could be good business for the lawyers, but they are sceptical about whether lawyers or judges are well-equipped to handle rights cases. For them, the root of the problem is the imbalance in political power, and 'major surgery to the body politic' is the answer they provide. Hence the growing interest in such things as a different electoral system, an elected second chamber, freedom of information legislation and an overhaul of the judiciary. By comparison, a bill of rights is to them little more than a 'cosmetic'.

Of course, the guarantees provided by such a bill are only worth what society is prepared to accept; its existence is of little use unless protection is extended to all groups, including unpopular minorities. The absence of such a document may not matter if society feels the rights should exist. Tampering with constitutional arrangements may be useful to remedy an obvious deficiency, but it cannot be relied upon to correct all of society's wrongs. As one commentator has put it; 'At times, certainly, to paraphrase Cassius in *Julius Caesar*, 'the fault lies not in our institutions, but in ourselves'.

Other ideas

There are other things which can be done. Australia has had the Senate Standing Committee for the **Scrutiny of Bills** since 1981, and one of the criteria it has adopted in discussing the merits of bills is their infringement or otherwise of human rights. The Committee has a watching brief to alert the Senate to possible problems and to draw attention to those which need examination and reconsideration. Figures for the early years of its existence show that in about one third of cases, there was a clause or clauses which did not initially meet the criteria laid down.

Another possibility is the establishment of a **human rights commission**. A Labour lawyer, Sam Silkin, proposed such a commission more than 20 ago. In addition to backing the incorporation of the Convention into British law, he wanted such a body 'to investigate, report and recommend to Parliament, in the same way as does the [Ombudsman], but like him it would have no power to enforce' (quoted by Ewing and Gearty). Under his proposal, the Commission would have initially examined breaches of the incorporated Convention, and referred these to Parliament. The difficulty is that it may be Parliament which has itself passed the offending legislation under which the violation of rights has been found. If this has happened, it is uncertain that a government with a Parliamentary majority would be willing to change the law.

Such a Commission exists in Australia where it is charged with the task of promoting and protecting human rights. It reviews statutes and proposals for bills to ensure that they are consistent with the maintenance of human rights, and reports to the appropriate minister on its findings. It can also enquire into any area of government policy, and issue reports on areas where new legislation is necessary if the country is to ensure the protection of rights at home and compliance with international obligations undertaken by the country. Its wide-ranging powers also include responsibility for the operation of the anti-discriminatory legislation on grounds of gender and race. In carrying out its duties, the criterion it bears in mind is the need for the country to maintain the highest standard of commitment to human rights, and in particular to ensure that Australia meets its obligations in international law, primarily under its adherence to the ICCPR and other UN/ILO covenants.

Freedom of Information legislation is another possibility, indeed a likelihood with the publication of a White Paper in January 1998. Such statutes are becoming a defining characteristic of accountable democratic government in many countries, but the idea has not as yet been embraced in Britain. The cult of secrecy – what the former Labour minister, Richard Crossman, once described as 'the British disease' – has few advantages, other than convenience to those in office. By contrast, if information is about to become available in the public domain, then judgements made by officials and ministers are likely to be more careful and considered lest they are seen to be acting unwisely. More than that, freedom of information is essential if the concept of a free press is to be meaningful. The right to independent publication needs to be matched by the ability to obtain the information which makes that freedom a reality, underpinned by a philosophy to be found outlined in James Madison's vision of representative government;

Knowledge will forever govern ignorance. And a people who mean to be their own governors must arm themselves with the power knowledge gives. A popular government without popular information or the means of acquiring it, is but a prologue to a farce or a tragedy, or perhaps both.

The Federalist Papers, no.10. 1787

We can learn from the experience of other countries. We have mentioned the experience of Australia, with its form of Senate Review and Human Rights Commission. In common with Canada and the USA, it has made great strides in recent years in working to improve its record on race relations. In all three countries there is now more emphasis on national unity. Everyone, whatever the origin of their families, is now seen as being alike in being Australian, Canadian or American.

A generation or more ago, the racial situation was very different in all three countries, America having its legacy of slavery and racial bitterness in the South, and Australia its much-criticised 'white Australia' policy. In all three cases, progress has been made, and whereas in the USA today it would not be uncommon to find a black manager of a major company, in Britain that is unlikely. In Australia and Canada, comments by politicians on the racial situation are likely to be less inflammatory than some made by our own representatives. It is not just a matter of legal rights, but also of changing the language of debate so that all can see the benefits of living in a multi-ethnic society.

Similarly with freedom of information. Australia and Canada have similar constitutional arrangements to our own, and yet government has been able to operate smoothly with greater openness. The US has gone further, and in 1978 the Civil Service Reform Act (the 'Whistleblowers Act') actually gave legal protection to those officials who reveal misconduct or malpractice. If they disclose any evidence of violation of the law, gross misuse of funds, or substantial danger to health or safety, they are protected from legal action or any other form of punishment such as demotion.

The possible solutions outlined above are not, of course, mutually exclusive. It is possible to have none, some or all or them, and for many who wish to see greater protection of rights and liberties a package of measures is desirable. In Britain, the Liberal Democrats want to incorporate the European Convention and proceed to develop a domestic Bill of Rights. They have also advocated the creation of a UK Commission of Human Rights empowered to assist complainants in bringing proceedings under the Bill of Rights, to bring proceedings to ensure compliance with its provisions, systematically to review law and practice in the sphere of civil liberties, and to recommend changes in existing law and practice. Under their proposal, it would have strong powers, and would replace the present Equal Opportunities Commission and the Commission for Racial Equality.

WHAT IS LIKELY TO BE DONE?

As we have seen, Labour has taken a bolder stand on matters of liberty in recent years. Even under Roy Hattersley, widely perceived as a constitutional conservative, there was a new determination to commit the party to a wide-ranging programme of constitutional reform and civil liberty legislation. The measures outlined gradually developed in the 1990s, and thinking moved on from a charter of rights to support for incorporation of the European Convention – with later the prospect of a home-grown bill of rights. There are, of course, past blemishes in Labour's record in this area, but following the massive election victory its ministers offer the best hope of change.

The commitments in the 1997 Manifesto were to more open government based on a freedom of information act and an independent National statistical service, and a series of proposals to enhance the rights of citizens. Incorporation of the European Convention is seen as 'a floor, not a ceiling', and the intention is that Parliament will add to the rights safeguarded. Reforms will include an attempt to end unjustifiable discrimination wherever it exists, changes in the civil justice system and the provision of Legal Aid, the removal of unfairnesses in the immigration appeals procedure, along with new rights for asylum seekers. Secure in office, and free from the fear of any likely Parliamentary defeat, there is little excuse for inaction on these commitments, and the government seems resolved to push ahead in its early years with this part of its programme of constitutional renewal.

DEMOCRACY AND RIGHTS

Sir Isaiah Berlin once expressed his view of the liberal political tradition in this way:

No society is free unless it is governed by two inter-related principles; first that no power but only rights can be regarded as absolute, second that there are frontiers within which men should be inviolable.

Democrats would agree, for human rights are not negotiable. They cannot be dependent on the will of government. They are fundamental and inalienable, a reality with which every government must come to terms.

Democrats are likely to favour a society which respects its citizens. They will not wish to tolerate a situation in which information is concealed, privacy eroded, the weak are not trusted with dignity and respect, the administration of justice is sometimes less than fair or ineffective, freedom of expression is endangered, minority groups are the victims of discrimination, women are denied full access to opportunity and the state is all-powerful, not open to searching examination and lacking in regard for individual liberty.

The overlap of democratic values and a concern for rights is explicitly recognised in the Preamble to the European Convention, with its reference to the fact that:

Fundamental freedoms...are best maintained on the one hand by an effective political democracy and on the other by a common understanding and observance of the Human Rights upon which they depend.

A democracy is more likely to protect essential rights, although this is not always the case. John Stuart Mill and other political philosophers have appreciated that there are inherent dangers in the concept of majority rule. All too easily, it can be associated with a lack of respect for a minority group, the more so if it is an unpopular one. This position was recognised in the judgement of the European Court in the case of Young, James and Webster (1982), three men who were protesting about their unjust dismissal for not joining a trade union:

Although individual interests must on occasion be subordinated to those of a group, democracy does not simply mean that the views of a majority must always prevail; a balance must be achieved which ensures the fair and proper treatment of minorities and avoids any abuse of a dominant position.

Rights campaigners would argue that we need to develop a culture of liberty in this country, but Ewing and Gearty claim that this flows from democracy and that the problem is that we lack a truly democratic culture (*Freedom under Thatcher*). Others also point to the absence of an attachment to democratic values, and a recent Liberal Democrat statement of 'Themes and Values' observes that:

A society without citizenship rights is not a true political community. Its members are not citizens, but subjects. They may have liberties, but in the deepest sense they are not free. And that is precisely the position in this country.

A society in which individuals are given opportunities to pursue their aims and lifestyles, develop their talents and fulfil their potential free from unnecessary interference is one in which freedom reigns. In Britain, that freedom depends not on any constitution or written guarantee, but on our traditional attachment to liberty which we expect Parliament and courts to defend. It may have provided us with a situation which is preferable to that in many other countries, but in the

1990s many people are aware that there are few grounds for complacency. When rights can be taken from some people, the freedom of the whole community is under threat.

Revision Hints

Check on the British record on rights and their protection. Note the differing verdicts of those who have studied the subject, and decide whether there is a problem of inadequate means of redress. If there is a problem of non-recognition of rights in Britain, does it amount to a 'crisis'? Might such a crisis be resolved by the incorporation of the Convention, or is the protection it offers now rather deficient? Do we need a new bill of rights, or are there better alternative means of protecting rights available – for instance, via freedom of information legislation, or the conferring of new positive rights such as Labour preferred a few years ago?

Examination Hints

Many questions have been mentioned elsewhere, but having read through all the material presented it should be possible to tackle the issues better now. Think not only about the content to be included in your answer, but about the wording of the question and how you might best tailor your response to its precise wording. Take a question such as this: **'How adequately do British judges handle issues of civil liberties?'**

In answering such a question, consider the opening words 'How adequately'. Like other phrases such as 'To what extent', this requires a judgement of scale. It is not appropriate to write down all you know about the topic without any assessment. In their reports, Chief Examiners often allude to the way in which strong candidates focus on the words that identify the skill that they are called upon to demonstrate, and may even refer to such key words in their concluding paragraph as a means of pointing out the relevance of their answer. 'How adequately' requires a case to be stated for and against. Both sides will need examples to illustrate the arguments. It is preferable to argue the case you most support after you have dealt with the other viewpoint, and logically the one you favour should include more (or more convincing) examples than for the side you wish to oppose.

In the question we have chosen

1 You might at the beginning talk about the role of judges (to interpret and enforce the law in an impartial manner; they should protect the rights of the citizen and of the state, according to the rule of law).

2 You might then decide to state the arguments against the view that judges support civil liberties.

3 In favour of the view that judges support civil liberties, you might make the point that sometimes the law which they are being asked to enforce actually constrains civil liberties.

4 Moving towards the conclusion you could mention that in recent years, judges have spoken out strongly in favour of a bill of rights and/or the European Convention (eg Lords Scarman and Taylor), some have been influenced more by 'European' thinking in their judgements, and many of the leading judicial figures have showed an increasing spirit of independence over a range of policy areas.

Group Work

You are now able to discuss the issues raised in matters of rights under several headings such as:

- What do we mean by rights?
- What are the most important freedoms?
- How are they protected in Britain, and what limitations are imposed upon them?
- Did the balance of the relationship between the individual and the state significantly change in the years after 1979?
- Are new laws necessary to protect rights in Britain? Should any old laws be reformed?
- What new forms of protection are necessary or desirable?

By now, we have seen the likely **Practice Questions** and come across the key words which have featured in past **Glossaries**.

Further Reading and References

Berlin, I., 1969 'Two concepts in liberty' in *Four essays on Liberty*, Oxford , OUP

Ewing and Gearty, (1990) *Freedom under Thatcher*, Oxford, Clarendon Press

Klug, Starmer and Weir, (1996) *The Three Pillars of Liberty*, London, Routledge

Rowntree Reform Trust, (1995), *State of the Nation* poll. Full details available from MORI

Sieghart, P., (1988) *Human Rights in the UK*, Clarendon Press

INDEX